57 Ways To Get New Clients:
A Guide for Tax Professionals

Edward A. Lyon, JD, CTM

John D. Pollock, CTM

Tax Master Network, LLC
2619 Erie Avenue
Cincinnati OH 45208
www.TaxMasterNetwork.com

57 Ways to Get New Clients

Copyright © 2018 by Financial Gravity Companies, Inc.

All rights reserved. No part of this book may be reproduced or transmitted in any form or by any means without written permission from the author.

Introduction

In 2005, Keith VandeStadt and I launched the software program that became the foundation of the Tax Master Network. We wanted to give tax professionals a planning and presentation system they could use to give their clients the savings they *really* wanted. Our first members loved the system, and many of them are still with us, 13 years later. They immediately saw how our approach filled a need for proactive planning tools. Several of them even told us, "if you hadn't come up with your system, I would have had to do it myself."

We expected our members to bombard us with questions about using our new software. But that was never a problem. Instead, they wanted to know how we could help them sell their new service. How could they introduce proactive tax planning to clients who were used to old-school compliance services? How could they use tax savings to lure new clients to their practice?

So, we took the advice we offer in Strategy #32 ("Listen") and we created marketing tools and resources. We created seminar kits, marketing postcards, and template prospecting letters.

Members told us which materials worked and which didn't. So, we listened some more, and took the advice in Strategy #5 ("Test and measure") and refined them. We kept what worked and learned what we could from what didn't work so we could improve it.

Today, the Tax Master Network community includes hundreds of tax and finance professionals from across the country. Every week we host a Member Call-In where members share their successes (and occasional failures).

Together, we learn more effective ways to get the clients we want.

Paul Simon may have taught us "50 Ways to Leave Your Lover," but we've learned there are far more than 50 ways to get new clients.

This book represents the collective wisdom of those years and that national community. You'll find practical advice, effective strategies and tactics you can start using *today*, without spending a dime, to build the business of your dreams.

Are you just launching your practice? If so, you'll find all the strategies you need in this one little book.

Are you bored with your practice, looking to reinvent yourself with new, more affluent clients? If that's the case, you'll learn how to refine your existing marketing to attract the new clients you crave.

When you're finished reading, if you like what you see, we invite you to visit our website and sign up for our weekly newsletter. Just visit www.TaxMasterNetwork.com and enter your email for more great strategies like the ones in this book.

Here's wishing you good luck on your journey and thanking you for letting us join you!

#1: Have a Marketing Mindset

If you're like most tax professionals, you think you're in the business of preparing taxes for people. Maybe you're also in the business of planning their taxes, or even resolving IRS problems.

That's a perfectly natural assumption. Unfortunately, it's also wrong.

Like it or not, you're really in the business of convincing people to *pay* you to prepare their taxes, or plan their taxes, or solving their IRS problems.

I don't know how much you know about taxes. I don't know how clever you are at spotting opportunities to save. I have no idea how effective you are at negotiating with auditors. Truth be told, I don't even care about any of that.

But what I do know, beyond a shadow of a doubt, is that none of that knowledge, none of that cleverness, and none of that silver-tongued negotiation means anything if you don't have clients to work for.

Most tax professionals go into business to "do" taxes. They get up in the morning thinking about the work they have to do that day, the returns they might have to prepare, the notices they might have to respond to. That's fine. Those are all important, and if you don't do the work you promise, you won't be in business long.

But if that's *all* you think about, you're doomed to stay small. The key to getting the clients you need to grow your practice – or getting the "better" clients you need to "upgrade" your practice – is marketing. When you switch from thinking of yourself as the *provider* of your service to the *marketer* of your service, you'll be well on your way to building the practice of your dreams.

John's Comments – As you work your way through this book and begin to create the Marketing Mindset necessary for your success, consider what it is you are selling. Are you selling a commodity that someone can get cheaper somewhere else? Are you selling a result? Are you selling something they value? Why do they value it? What do you offer that allows you to stand apart in an ocean of over 800,000 CPAs, EAs and other accounting professionals?

#2: Focus On Your Marketing Funnel

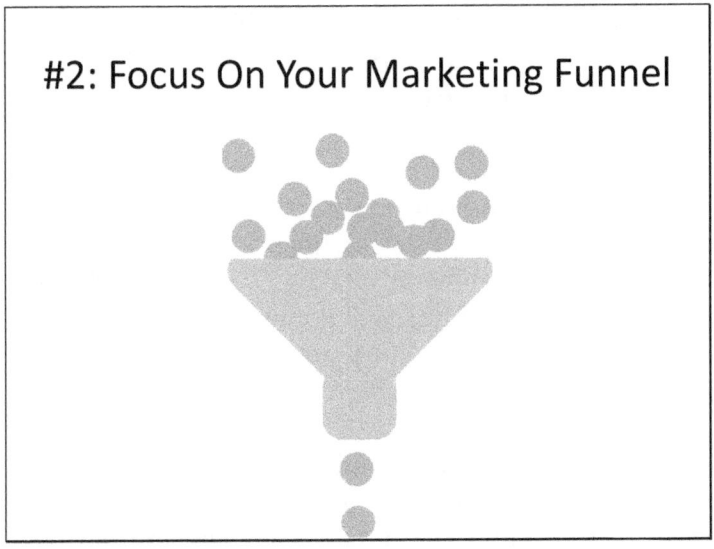

Marketing works a lot like a funnel. In fact, marketing professionals often speak of creating a funnel. You start by pouring leads into the top, nurture them with ongoing marketing over time, and see how many of them drop through the bottom as clients.

The funnel analogy works because not all the leads you pour into the top will end up becoming clients. And that's fine. Really, it is.

Too many tax professionals have a *sales* focus, rather than a *marketing* focus. They meet a prospective client and think they must close him. If not, they hang their head in failure. If it happens too often, they get really depressed. That's just silly. Nobody closes everyone they meet! (And if you do, you're not challenging yourself enough.)

The most experienced and most effective tax professionals focus on generating leads, then letting the funnel do the work. Want more clients? Feed more leads into the funnel.

It's OK if your "closing ratio" is just 20-30% — because doubling the number of *leads* will still eventually mean twice as many new *clients*.

An effective marketing funnel gives you more chances to close the same lead. Someone's not ready to hire you now? No problem! Put them on your email list. Send them your weekly email for as long as it takes. *Someday* they'll be in enough pain over their taxes that they'll be ready to hire someone – and there you'll be, after building credibility and rapport the whole time.

Legendary football coach Lou Holtz once said, "in this world, if you're not growing, you're dying." Focusing on an effective marketing funnel is a great way to make sure you keep growing.

John's Comments – Think of your funnel as sorting cherries. You want the funnel to kick out the ripe cherries immediately, so you can eat them before they go bad (we have a saying internally that new leads are cut flowers, contact them before they die, but I am now mixing metaphors). The green cherries need time to ripen, (keep reading for more on this) and there will always be pits, just discard and move on. This is a lot to ask of a funnel, but good markets expect this kind of sorting to be built into the process.

#3: Market All Year Long

Tax professionals are acutely aware of the calendar. Everyone in America knows what April 15 means. So, much of our marketing revolves around that date. Watch any sporting event in January or February and you'll see ads for H&R Block. Drive past any strip mall that same time of year and you'll see a foam rubber Statue of Liberty dancing on the curb.

Are you focusing your own marketing on that same period of time? Here's the problem. Block and Liberty have taken advantage of Strategy #5 to learn those are the best times to attract their core 1040-filer clients eager to claim their refunds. But that may not be the best time to attract *your* clients at all! Business owners may not have records ready to file early, or, if they know they owe, may simply prefer to wait. Investors may prefer to wait until later in the season when they feel confident they have their *final* amended 1099s.

Other clients may be stuck waiting on K1s that won't appear until after Labor Day. These are generally the "better" clients that build a better practice – and many of them may not even be in the market for tax services on April 15.

Here's another problem with starting and stopping your marketing: you can't start and stop your bills. Office rent is due every month. Your mortgage and car payment are due every month. Your kids want to eat every *day*.

Do you really want to be one of those squirrelly tax professionals who works 80-hour weeks all winter to store up enough nuts to live the rest of the year? (It's fine if you do, but most of us don't.) Or would you rather bring in a steady stream of year-round clients and year-round billings?

Not sure how to do that? Read on.

John's Comments – Outsiders consider a tax professional as someone that only works 2 months a year. We know better. Have you considered creating a marketing campaign around all key tax times and inserting other things you do at that time to remind them you are not just numbers in boxes?

#4: Create *Systems* to Do the Work

Marketing can be hard work. (It can be lots of fun, too, but it's still work.) That's why it's so important to create systems to do all that work for you.

Michael Gerber, author of *The E-Myth* book series, says that most business owners (including most tax business owners) aren't really entrepreneurs. They're technicians, who were seized by an entrepreneurial impulse, who opened their own businesses, and who now do the same sort of work for their clients as they used to do for their employers. They run *practices*, not *businesses*.

There's nothing wrong with that, of course. But if you want to make the leap from owning a practice to owning a business, you'll need to create systems to do the work. In fact, Gerber argues, the most valuable work a business owner can ever do is to create systems to manage that work.

Here are some examples of the kinds of systems you can create to do your marketing:

- Use CRM software to automate the sales funnel we discussed in Strategy #3.

- Create scripts and ticklers for managing different marketing and advertising campaigns.

- Create scripts for the person who answers the phone to "sell" appointments to meet with you.

- Create ticklers to remind you to ask for referrals (Strategy #50) and quantify your value (Strategy #51).

- Create scripts for the staffer who bills for tax returns to gather client testimonials.

- Automate your weekly client emails.

Think hard enough and you'll probably think of a dozen more routine marketing functions that you can systematize. The more you automate, the more effective your marketing will be – and the more time you'll have for the actual "face time" that counts the most.

John's Comments - We use Infusionsoft and MS Dynamics. We consider Infusionsoft to be our PRM, Prospect Relationship Management and we Dynamics for Customer Relationship Management,

#5: Test and Measure

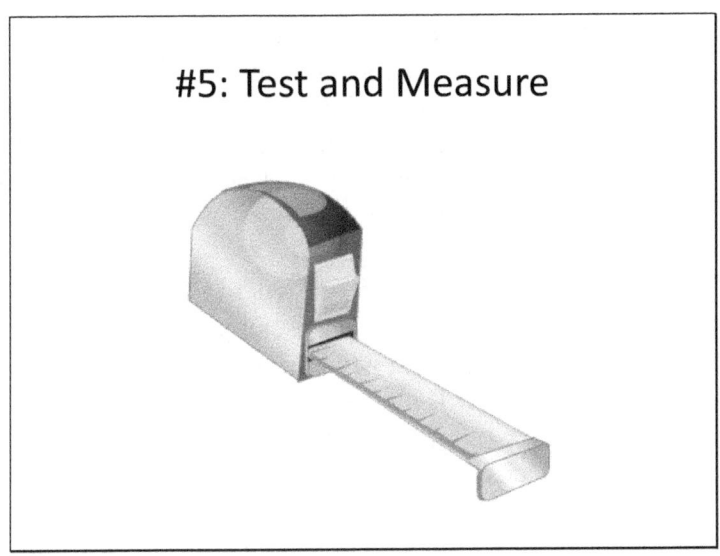

Got a great marketing idea?

Want to know if it's a smart idea or a waste?

Test it!

When you think of "marketing," you probably think of the creative work that goes into selling. You know, Don Draper and the gang from *Mad Men*, sitting around the office late at night in suits, chain-smoking and guzzling scotch, then putting together a great presentation to "wow" the client.

But smart marketers don't stop with the creative. They test their marketing and measure their results. How many new customers do they get in one market versus another? What's the return on investment (ROI) for a campaign in Cincinnati versus a campaign in Indianapolis?

Knowing your "metrics" is the key to evaluating any marketing campaign. This includes activities that you might not even think of as "campaigns." Strategy #56, for example, involves taking clients to lunch to generate referrals. You'll want to track how much you spend, along with how much revenue those referrals generate, just like you would track your return on investment in direct mail or online pay-per-click advertising.

Most business owners can tell you where they *think* their business comes from. But very few can pinpoint it with any real accuracy. Tracking and measuring your marketing is an essential step towards making the most of your efforts. Don't launch a campaign without knowing how you'll determine its success and cost-effectiveness.

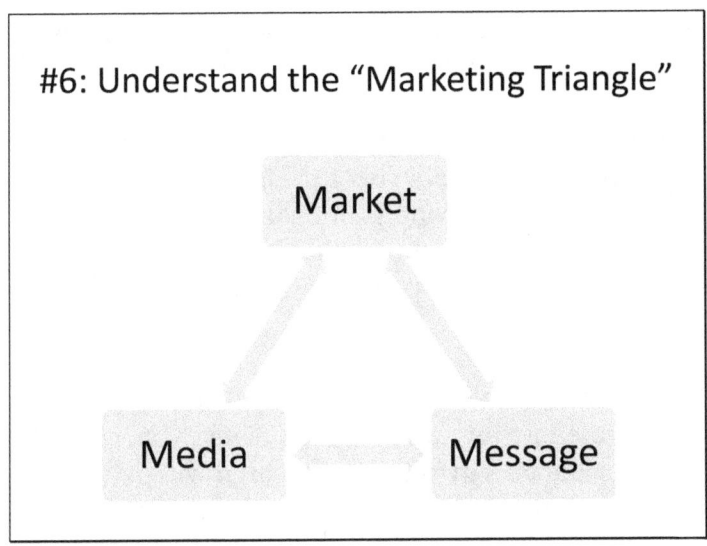

Too many tax professionals hear the word "marketing" and immediately think about media. Seminars? Direct mail? Print advertising? But in fact, the marketing process starts long before you decide on your media. And if you don't build your marketing on a solid foundation, you won't be nearly as effective with any media.

Here at the Tax Master Network, we talk about the "marketing triangle." Think of it as a three-legged stool that incorporates everything you need for successful campaigns:

- First, there's your actual "market." Who's your target? Who do you want to work for? What service do you want to provide? What value do you want to deliver? It all starts with "who." And the better you understand that "who," the more effective all your efforts will be.

- Next, there's your "message." What message do you want to deliver to your chosen market? What combination of features and benefits will arouse their curiosity and interest? What value can you promise to convince them to do business with you?

- Finally, *after* you've identified your market and crafted your message, there's your "media." What's the best platform for delivering your chosen message to your chosen market? What combination of factors will let you deliver it as inexpensively as possible to the widest possible audience?

You wouldn't sit on a stool if you saw that one or more of the legs were missing, would you? (Would you?) So why would you launch a marketing campaign without addressing all three points of the marketing triangle?

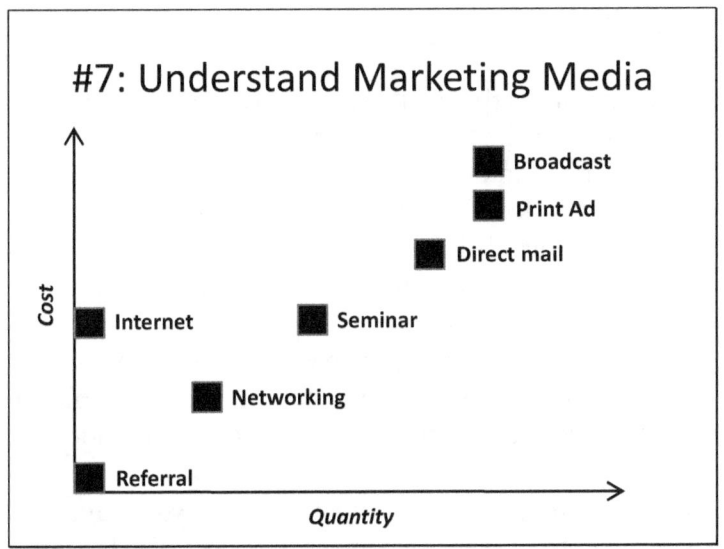

When you sit down to evaluate marketing media, there are two main issues to consider. First, how much does it cost? And second, how many people will it reach? You can even graph them out according to those two dimensions. So let's take a quick look at each of these marketing methods and see where they lie:

- You probably don't think of referrals as a marketing medium. But word-of-mouth is the most basic marketing medium you can use. It doesn't have to cost anything, which makes it ideal for new practices and practices where money is tight. But it also generally doesn't reach as far as other media.

- Here at the Tax Master Network, we define networking (like Chamber of Commerce meetings, Rotary clubs, and BNI lead groups) as the next step outward on the media graph. They don't cost a lot, and they give a greater reach than relying on your own personal contacts.

- The internet is the next step out. By "internet," we mean your website and your social media presence. Some sort of internet presence is almost mandatory these days. However, it's easy to overdo the internet and fool yourself into *thinking* you're working – especially with social media.

- Many Tax Master Network members use seminars to build their business. For my money, seminars offer the most attractive combination of low cost and wide reach.

- Direct mail gives you as much reach as you want, for a significantly larger investment. However, it also lets you home in on your ideal target prospect, as often as you're willing to mail.

- Print and broadcast advertising reach the widest quantity of prospects, but at the highest cost. The lure of all those eyeballs can be seductive – but most independent tax practices have a hard time making the economics work

Your challenge is to figure out which media will work best for your chosen market(s) and your chosen message(s). If you're looking for a particular type of business owners, referrals might be all you need. If you're looking for new movers, you might choose direct mail. And if you want to target a new professional market, you might ask an existing client or two to refer you to their professional association.

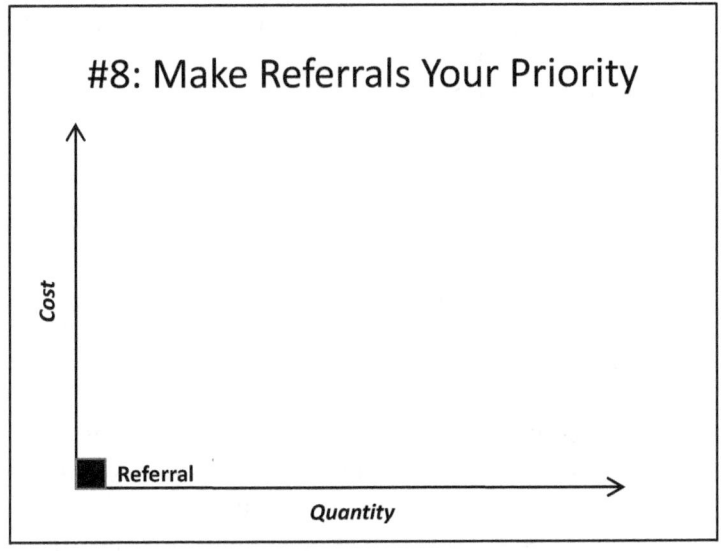

This may come as disappointing news to those of you who picked up this book looking for the latest "power closes" or social media strategies, but for most of you, good old-fashioned referrals may be all you need. All you're missing is the *systems* for generating them.

If you're like most tax professionals, referrals are already your most important source of new business. Let's take a look at why this is true, and why referrals make the best clients:

1. Referrals are *easier* to close. They're predisposed to know you, like you, and (especially) trust you, simply because they're referred by someone who already *does* know you, like you, and trust you.

2. Referrals are *faster* to close. The "learning curve" is shorter and the sales cycle is faster. You create instant authority works through your referral source. You generally just don't have to wait as long to close the deal with a referral.

3. Referrals are generally more willing to pay *higher fees*. The same credibility that helps you close them faster and easier also helps you charge more because you're no longer a commodity.

4. Referrals are more willing to give you *more referrals* themselves. They're more familiar with doing business through referrals. They're more comfortable with the process and they're more comfortable with the value. If someone comes to you via referral, they're more likely to "pay it forward" and refer new clients themselves.

Finally, you should be aware that some prospects will *only* do business with referrals. Generally, the higher you move up the financial food chain, the less important and less effective any type of "cold" marketing will be. The clients you *really* want – the folks you read about in your local business journal's "Top 100 Leaders" section – won't *ever* go looking for you online. If they need a new tax pro, they'll ask someone as affluent as they are for a referral.

Makes sense, right?

So, why don't more tax professionals think of "referrals" as a marketing strategy? Why don't more of them focus on creating systems to generate them?

Referrals are so important that we'll focus the last eight strategies on getting more of them. Until then, I just want you to re-orient your brain and think of "referrals" as your primary marketing medium.

John's Comments – A super simple and free strategy is to put, "we appreciate referrals" in your signature line of your e-mail.

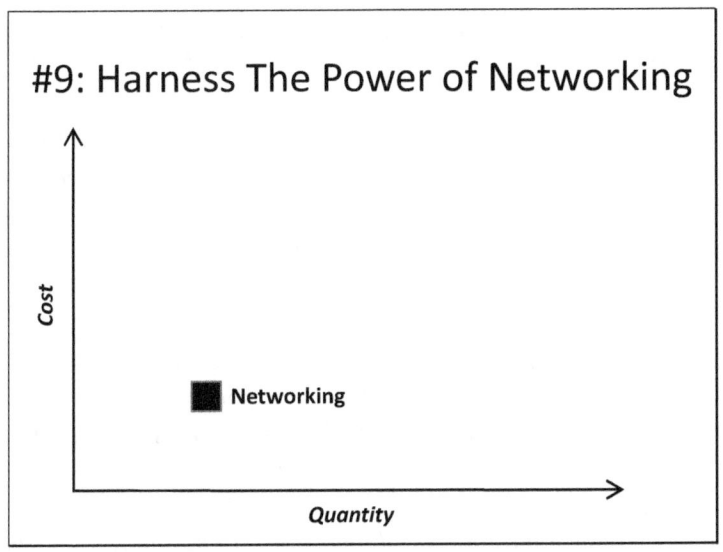

#9: Harness The Power of Networking

If referrals from clients aren't enough to get you where you want to go, networking (which we'll define here as introductions from people who *aren't* actual clients) lets you take your message to the streets, easily and inexpensively. Networking is also crucial for new tax businesses when you don't have an existing clientele.

Networking is cheap. It doesn't have to cost anything at all. You don't get the same reach as with seminars, print advertising, or broadcast advertising. But starting the personal connection you get with a networking introduction outweighs the reach you get with any kind of marketing where you start out as a stranger.

The key to networking is quickly appealing to your listener's desire to be a *hero*. You want to be able to dangle some sort of bait, in 30 seconds or less, that gets your listener to think "who do I know who would be impressed with me if I introduced them." It's like the elevator speech that we'll talk about in Strategy #27, except you're delivering it indirectly.

There's no shortage of groups you can join specifically for networking – think professional associations, Chambers of Commerce, Rotary clubs, and "leads groups" like BNI. But lots of networking happens informally, too, when people's guards are down, such as at your kids' soccer games.

Make it a point to introduce yourself to someone new every day, even in the busiest part of tax season. Before you've met the full second dozen, it will be a habit. And with it, you'll be amazed at how fast your business grows.

John's Comments – Remember my comments and questions in #1? This is where it is important. Many of these groups allow for an introduction, #27 will help with this.

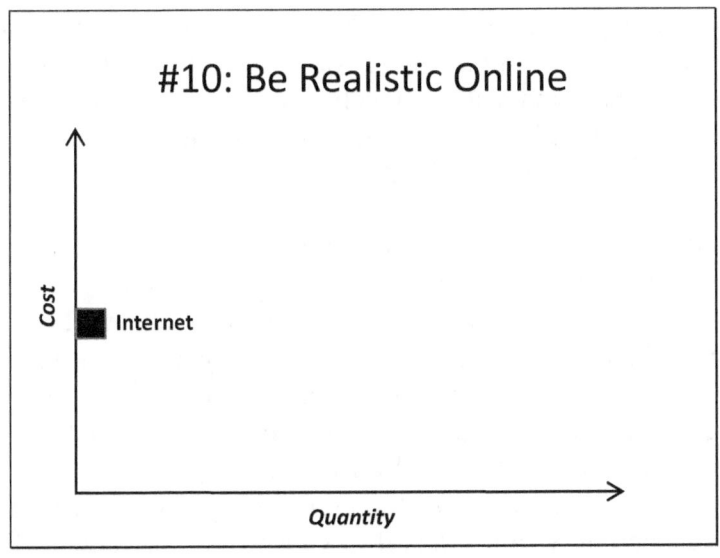

You can't open a professional journal these days without seeing something about internet marketing. Social media, especially, is a white-hot topic. And the internet is an important part of most tax professionals' marketing. It's easy to be seduced by the lure of new media. But putting up a pretty website, managing a Facebook fan page, and tweeting abut taxes may not contribute nearly as much to your bottom line as you think. If you're serious about building your business, you'll want to be ruthless about testing and measuring your results, in terms of time as well as money.

You need a website. That's a given. Even if all you do to market is solicit referrals, prospects will want a place where they can go to do their "due diligence" on you. We'll talk in Strategy #29 about what that site should accomplish.

Many Tax Master Network members experiment (and succeed) with pay-per-click advertising. That's worth a try if your target market is the right demographic to be looking for your service online. So, if you're looking for young professionals and tech-savvy clients, by all means test pay-per-click. But if you're looking for older, more affluent clients, you'll probably be disappointed.

And then there's social media. We have a *very* small number of members who have succeeded in using Facebook and other social media to get new clients. The ones who do are generally targeting a very specific kind of prospect who uses social media extensively themselves. But most members who experiment in this arena find that social media is more useful for maintaining existing contacts and relationships than for finding new ones. Social media certainly can be a part of your marketing funnel. But pay attention to the time you spend online – it's really easy to fool yourself into thinking you're working when it's just not an effective use of your time.

We've also experienced success with advertising on social media networks. When it works, it's because it lets you target incredibly specific prospects. Interested in left-handed, red-headed chiropractors? From 37-42 years old? In a specific three-county region? You can do that! There might not be many of them. But you can reach them! In fact, the Tax Master Network has a done-for-you marketing program that can put this power to work for you.

John's Comments – Once again referencing #1, the internet will become very expensive, very quick if you don't have a solution or value-based message or market more targeted than, "someone that needs tax help."

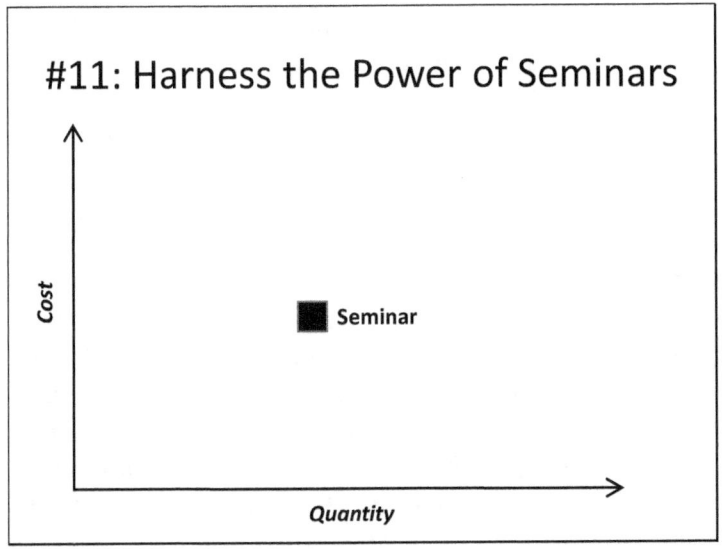

#11: Harness the Power of Seminars

For my money, seminars are the fastest and easiest way to leverage your marketing efforts by getting in front of *groups* of prospects at the same time.

Selling individual clients is a bit like hand-to-hand combat. Pouring leads into your marketing funnel, one by one by one, can take time and effort. Many of those leads will eventually fall out of the funnel as clients. But that process can take time.

Sometimes, you just want to dump a lot of leads into the top of your funnel at once. Seminars are the best way to generate quantities of *qualified* leads for that funnel.

One former member had focused his entire business on business owners in his town north of Atlanta. A local financial planner asked him to speak for a group of nurse-anesthetists. Our member used that single appearance to springboard into a series of seminars to state and local associations throughout the southeast. That one presentation was enough to create an entirely new clientele!

John's Comments – I believe Seminars have reached a tipping point. When I started in financial services I could fill two seminars of 40 each from a 5000-piece mailing in 2002. When I stopped doing them I was mailing 10,000 pieces and barely getting 20 for one seminar. But, the over saturation of annuity product seminars means that results dropped precipitously, now the market is opening up again. But, a different message (not pushing high commission insurance products) to the right people (consider reading <u>Selling Tax Plans</u> book) to the right audience (know your target) and this could be huge. Also, there are dozens of places you can speak for free. Finally, there are 'speaking bureaus' that specialize is placing speakers in local and regional Rotaries, Chamber and other similar groups.

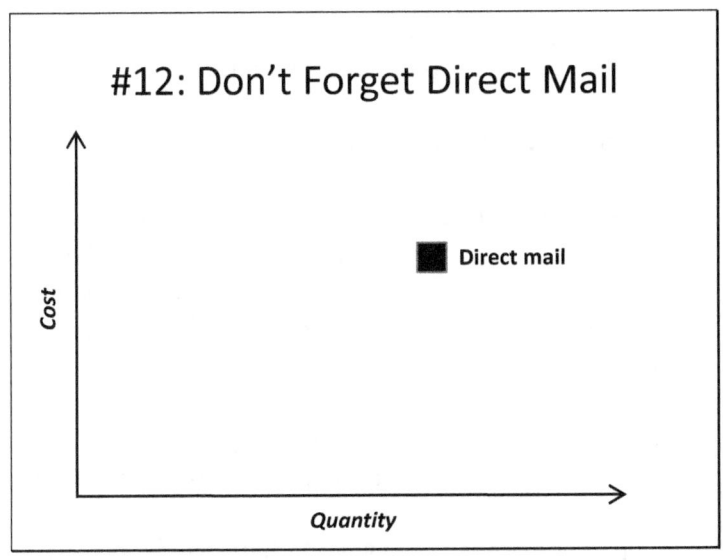

In this age of electronic everything, it's easy to forget old-school "junk mail." But it still arrives in your mailbox every day, doesn't it? That's because it still works. The keys to making direct mail work, though, are targeting your list and matching your message to that target. You can't simply decide to throw a couple grand at a direct mail campaign and expect any kind of success.

Here are three questions you need to consider up front:

- **Who do you want to reach?** Be as specific as possible. How old are they? How much do they make? Where do they live? What reason might they have to be interested in your service? If you're targeting business owners, for example, do you want to target startups? (They may not have a tax relationship already, but also may not have enough income to afford you.) Do you want established businesses with a decade or more of longevity behind them? (They probably can afford you, but they might have a longstanding tax relationship that no direct-mail piece can get them to consider leaving.)

- **Can you rent (or, better yet, compile) a list of them to mail to?** Can you combine two or more lists to narrow down your market? (For example, merging lists of business owners who also subscribe to *The Wall Street Journal* will give you a different target than business owners who subscribe to *ESPN: The Magazine*.)

- **How accurate is that list?** You've probably seen yourself on at least one list where you don't belong!

Once you have your list, your next challenge is to craft a mailer that actually gets *read* and captures their attention. We recommend using postcards to drive them to a website. Not only is a postcard the lowest-cost option, a message on a postcard (as opposed to a message on a letter inside an envelope) catches their eye immediately, even if your recipient sorts their mail over the recycling bin. One bold promise can get them to put aside the card and visit your website, where you can engage them with longer copy, photos, and even video.

Direct mail also lets you test and measure different campaigns more accurately than just about any other media. You get a list of all your prospects up front, so you can be confident that a client coming from that list came from that campaign. You can test a campaign with a small part of a list before spending more to roll the campaign out to the rest.

Last tip: if you can afford, say, 3,000 pieces, you'll do better by mailing the same 1,000 people three times than you will by mailing 3,000 people once. You'll thank me.

John's Comments – This is another tipping point solution. As email rose, snail mail dropped. The mail box has never been emptier. I only get medical bills in the mail all bills are electronic or on autopay. I am not the exception. But, this means the opportunity to engage the mailbox is great! Lists are better and there are now services online that will allow you to set up and mail paper easier than email.

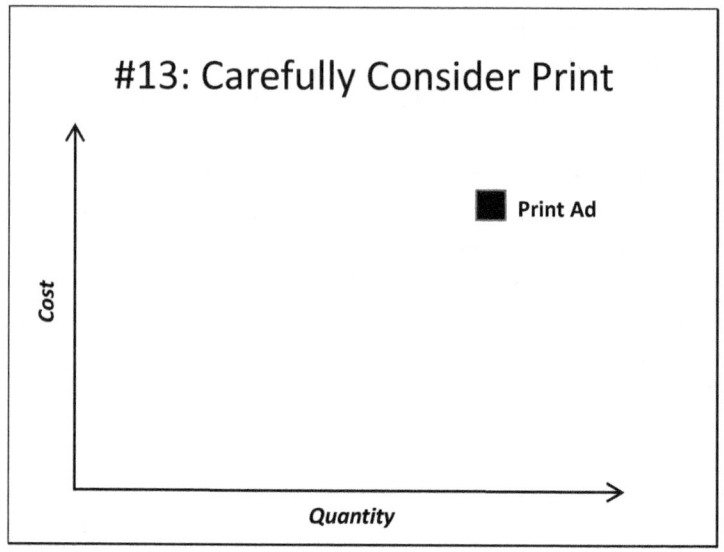

Print advertising lets you reach a far larger audience than any of the media we've discussed so far. But it generally costs a lot more. And unless you've got an especially targeted publication, most of those "eyeballs" will have no interest in your service at all. So, you have to be careful, because you'll have to pay to reach all those eyeballs whether they have any value to you or not!

You'll need to consider these factors and more before bucking up for a print campaign:

- Who exactly are you targeting? What publications do they read and trust? (Approaching them in the local business journal will give you different results than approaching them in the local bridal publication.)

- What part of those publications do they read? When and how often do they read them? (You might actually do better attracting business owners in the sports section than the financial page.)

- What do you want them to do when they see your ad? Pick up the phone? Visit your website?

Once you've narrowed in on your target market's reading habits, that's where *testing* and *measuring* come in. You need to know exactly how much a client is worth and how much you're willing to pay to acquire one. Then, you can set aside a small budget to test print advertising and measure your results before you invest more in a broader campaign.

Finally, don't be conned by advertising salespeople telling you "you have to advertise over and over to build your 'brand' so that when our readers need you, they'll know who you are." Remember, they get paid for selling ads, *not* for growing your business!

That sort of ongoing image campaign might make sense if you were a bigger company with a bigger advertising budget. (Actually, it wouldn't – I'm just being nice to the ad sales reps.) But it's an expensive indulgence for an independent tax business. You'll do much better to capture leads through less expensive media and feed them into the top of your marketing funnel, then use your own channels (like the weekly email we discuss in Strategy #57) to work them over time.

John's Comments – Be careful of what I call "pay-to-play" print. In other words, they will "let" you write an article for the local paper, magazines, etc. IF you advertise. See #19 for better options.

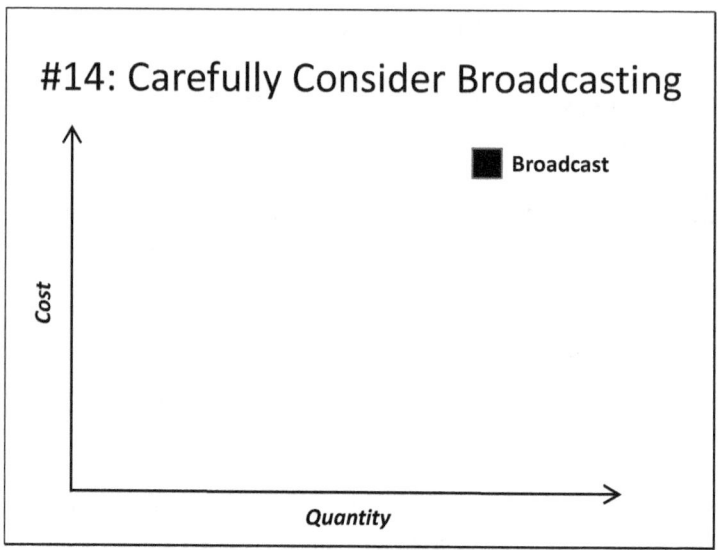

Radio and television give you the greatest possible reach. But they're also generally the most expensive marketing media. And they have the same problem as print advertising – most of the eyeballs and ears you reach will have no interest in your service. So, are they worth the cost?

In most cases, the economics just don't work for local tax businesses. H&R Block can afford to advertise because they're aggregating the buying power of 12,000 offices and spreading it over 24 million broadly working-class and middle-class target clients. Local practices, especially those targeting business owners and affluent 1040 filers, just can't match that.

However, television and radio *can* be a part of your marketing mix, *if* you get the right price (particularly on local cable), and *if* you leverage your television spots throughout the rest of your marketing:

- Drop your commercial into your website where visitors can watch.

- Broadcast your commercial in a loop with video testimonials and video "Q & A" sessions in your office lobby. (See Strategy #23, "Video Sells.")

- Include a screenshot of your television appearance in your brochures, folders, and other written materials.

- Make sure the headline or slogan in your broadcast ads is the same as in your other material.

Most tax business owners won't ever use broadcast television or radio in their marketing. That's fine. The Big Four don't advertise there. White-shoe law firms don't advertise there. Few physicians or dentists advertise there, either. But unless you're looking to build a high-volume business with "middle America" clients, it's just more firepower than you need.

John's comment – Cable can be surprisingly inexpensive (compared to other broadcast media) and you can target zones. But, you will probably only get Gen X and up age groups. Millennials don't have cable, they have Netflix and Hulu. Now services like SlingTV and YouTube allow for live TV. Also, production of the commercial can get pricey, but there are NO tax pros in this space.

#15: Target the Right Markets

Lots of tax professionals decide to go into business for themselves . . . hang out a shingle . . . and start taking whatever clients they can drag through the door. They joke about "targeting" anyone who can fog a mirror, or (hopefully) anyone whose check clears.

Twenty years down the road, they wake up one morning, look at their client list, and realize they spent those 20 years building a practice they don't want! (That's exactly what brings so many experienced professionals to the Tax Master Network – to reinvent their practice with a whole new clientele.)

The good news is, you can avoid that sad fate – even if you're one of those *20-years-later* types.

The answer starts with targeting clients you actually *want* to work with and finding ways to fill your calendar with enough of them that you don't have to settle for one-offs, troublemakers, and other pains in your rear end.

Targeting your clients pays dividends in other ways, too:

- Targeting a specific clientele means you'll be able to take advantage of target-rich environments, like professional associations.

- Targeting your market means you can build a reputation within a tight-knit community, fostering referrals. If you become the "go-to" tax professional within that community, you'll be able to let that reputation do your marketing for you.

- Targeting a market can give you enough experience with those clients to make your actual work easier. If you target chiropractors, for example, you'll soon become so familiar with their tax issues that you'll be able to "read" their tax returns as quickly as they read an x-ray. And that, of course, helps make you the "go-to" professional that everyone in the group clamors to work with.

John's comments – This is why the saying there is "riches in niches" exists. Sorry to the grammar police that pronounce niche properly, like quiche.

#16: Target the Right *Prospects*

You may think that after you've targeted a market or two or three, you can call it a day. Unfortunately, that's not enough. Once you've targeted the right markets, now it's time to target the right prospects *within* those markets.

Let's say you live in California and you're targeting real estate agents. There are thousands of agents scattered throughout the state. But most of them don't make much money. There are new agents just getting started, still hungry for their first commissions. There are struggling agents who just don't "get it" and won't be around much longer. There are semi-retired agents, no longer really marketing themselves, looking for a social life and an occasional commission from friends downsizing into retirement communities. Not all agents are created equal, and only a fraction of them are really worth pursuing.

What do you do? Do you join the local association and mail to all 3,000 agents on their list? Or do you compile a select list of the top 100 producers and mail something every month to build your name and credibility?

You've no doubt heard critics of income equality argue that America's wealth is tilted to "the top 1%," sometimes "the top 5%." It's important to realize that there's a 1%, or 5%, or 20%, in every market. And those are often (although not always) the ones you want to target.

Don't just look at your target markets as monoliths. Take the time to discover and understand the differences within those markets. The more tightly you can focus your market, the better you can match your message to that market – and the more effective you'll be with any medium.

#17: Make the Most of Your Affinities

When it comes to targeting markets, you'll do best if you can show your target some reason they should pick you over your competition. That means demonstrating your affinity to them.

When I launched my personal practice, I decided to target real estate agents. I had several reasons for picking them. For starters, they're all over the place. The successful ones make enough money that they need my help (and can afford my service). And they're reachable in groups, like agencies and associations, which was important because I wanted to prospect through seminars.

But there was one more important reason to target real estate agents – my mother was an agent herself. That gave me a perspective on their day-to-day work, their problems, and their frustrations that few of my competitors could understand. In short, the fact that I was an agent's son meant I could demonstrate an *affinity* for that particular market. I could *relate* to prospects in that market. And that affinity helped me land speaking engagements and clients in over 30 states across the country.

What sort of target markets can you demonstrate an affinity to? Here are just a few ideas:

- Did you have a career in another industry before becoming a tax professional? Target your former colleagues! (One of our most successful members was a real estate broker before becoming a tax professional – now she charges associations $2,500 for her tax-planning seminars.)

- Do you have a particular expertise from a previous career? Another one of our members worked for Toys'R'Us before opening his own practice. He targets independent retailers who *love* getting his expertise at a reasonable price.

- Are you an avid golfer? Target fellow golfers! (Your local club might have welcomed a seminar on deducting golf-related meals and entertainment, back when golf was still deductible!)

- Are you an immigrant or a child of immigrants? Target your fellow countrymen. (This is especially effective if you're looking for business clients, as many ethnic groups are more entrepreneurial than native-born Americans.)

You get the picture. Look for target markets who can identify with you, and watch your business grow!

#18: Speak Your Prospects' Language

Every group in America has a language of its own. Professional groups, ethnic groups, and even demographic groups all have their own "secret" language and words with "secret" meanings. (Try talking to your teenager without understanding the subtle shades of "like," and you'll be lost!)

If you can speak your target market's language yourself, you'll endear yourself to the group and its members in a way that almost nothing else can.

Do you work with healthcare professionals? Why would you "review" their tax returns and "recommend" changes when you can "diagnose" mistakes and "prescribe" solutions?

Do you work with mob bosses? Why offer to "cut" their taxes when you can "whack" them instead? (Okay, maybe not the best example! But I'm always angling for the laugh, and you get the idea.)

We have a member in Tulsa who works with real estate agents. A few years ago, I helped him create a set of three maintenance packages to offer those clients. We could have called them "silver," "gold," and "platinum" like everyone else. But real estate agents themselves target three sorts of buyers: "starter" home buyers, "move-up" home buyers, and "executive" homer buyers. So why wouldn't we name our member's maintenance packages to mirror his own prospects' markets?

Oh, and does he "prospect" for clients? Nope. He "farms," just like they do. Does he offer a "free tax Analysis?" Nope. He offers a "free Tax Appraisal."

You get the picture. Try to learn your market's "secret language," *speak* it, and watch the clients eat it up.

#19: Join Your Prospects' Associations

If your target market has an association, why on earth would you *not* join? Most professional associations have some sort of special "affiliate" membership. If not, they may still welcome you as a member. (Remember, professional associations themselves live or die by how well they market themselves to prospective members.)

- It gives you visibility and exposure. You can bet that few, if any, of your competitors go so far as to join outside groups.

- You may get the chance to sponsor a meeting, a class, or another event. This may include the chance to stand up and introduce yourself and the particular value you bring to the members.

- You may even get a chance to *teach* a class to your market. Imagine how powerful that implied endorsement will be in your chosen market! (For more information, see Strategy #20, below.)

Joining your market's association offers another, less obvious benefit – but one that can be even more important. Joining your market's association will help you *learn* about that market. You'll become more familiar with their work and their lives. You'll learn about their problems and their frustrations – and understanding a group's problems and frustration goes a long way towards demonstrating your affinity to the group.

Joining your market's association doesn't have to be limited to professional groups. You can target "subcultures" like athletes and sports fans, church members, and hobbyists of all sorts. My co-founder Keith is a "Detroit iron" aficionado and member of the 1961-62 Cadillac owners' group. I have no idea what commonalities fans of old tailfin Cadillacs might have to make them worth targeting as a tax clientele. But I know that if I wanted to target them, my first step would be to join their association!

John's Comment – Many associations have magazines, which is a type of print that makes more sense than the "pay-to-play" local paper.

#20: "Speak and Grow Rich"

I mentioned earlier that for my money, seminars give you the best combination of "reach" and "cost" of any marketing channel. Now I want to focus on one specific strategy – speaking at sponsored seminars.

The hardest part about delivering a seminar is assembling an audience. But that can be the easiest part if you get someone to do it for you. Right now, there are meeting planners across your town who are dying for great content. They manage sales agencies, associations, Chambers of Commerce, and similar groups. Every week, every month, every quarter, they meet – and someone has to do the talking! It might as well be you.

Getting sponsored to speak at one of those meetings puts you (sometimes literally) on a pedestal. When you appear in front of an audience, you're not a salesperson looking for clients. You're an authority. You're an expert. And you appear with the implied endorsement of the organization and meeting planner who invited you. That's a powerful advantage in perception that you'll have over any of your peers.

Here are more strategies for booking seminars that put you in front of new clients:

- Ask your clients to introduce you to the folks who book speakers for the groups and associations they belong to. If you're working with a real estate agent, for example, ask him or her to introduce you to the broker who runs the weekly office meeting and the president of the local association.

- Create a "one sheet" (one-page flyer) promoting your presentation. Be sure to appeal to the meeting planner and explain why appearing before his group will make him look good.

- Consider videotaping a presentation and posting it on your website. You'll gain immediate credibility just by doing so, and you can refer future seminar hosts to review you "in action."

The Tax Master Network offers five complete seminar kits with PowerPoint presentations and scripts ("Business Owners," "Real Estate Investors," "Tax Reform," and "Charitable Giving"). We also offer "mini-presentations" on specific topics like S corporations, medical expense reimbursement plans, and closely-held insurance companies. These are some of our most popular marketing resources, and members regularly tell us what great business builders those resources are for them.

John's comment – We have a speaker's agency we recommend to the Tax Master Network.

Once you're in front of an audience, there are three things you can do with them.

1. You can *educate* them. That's important – they come to your seminar to learn, and they'll feel ripped off if they don't walk away knowing something they didn't know before. But for your purposes, educating your audience may be the least important thing you can do.

2. You can *entertain* them. This is actually easier than you might think. Expectations are pretty low for "entertainment" in a tax seminar, so just letting a little personality shine through should do it. Remember, people want to do business with people they know, like, and trust. This is your chance to let them warm up to you.

3. Finally, you can *motivate* them. I don't care how much good information you give them. They'll forget half of it by the time they get home and the rest by the end of the day. If you don't motivate them to use that information to improve their lives, they may as well have spent the time watching TV or a movie. Your real goal in any speaking situation has to be to motivate your audience to do something with the information you present. And in most cases, of course, that "something" means doing business with you.

Please don't underestimate the importance of this strategy. Don't fall victim to thinking that prospecting through seminars is the same thing as teaching a class. If you need any further convincing, just think about this: the best-paid teacher at your kid's school drives a Honda, while successful salespeople (aka "motivators") drive new Jaguars and BMWs. Cynical? Yes. But true? Also yes.

#22: Book the Appointment *NOW!*

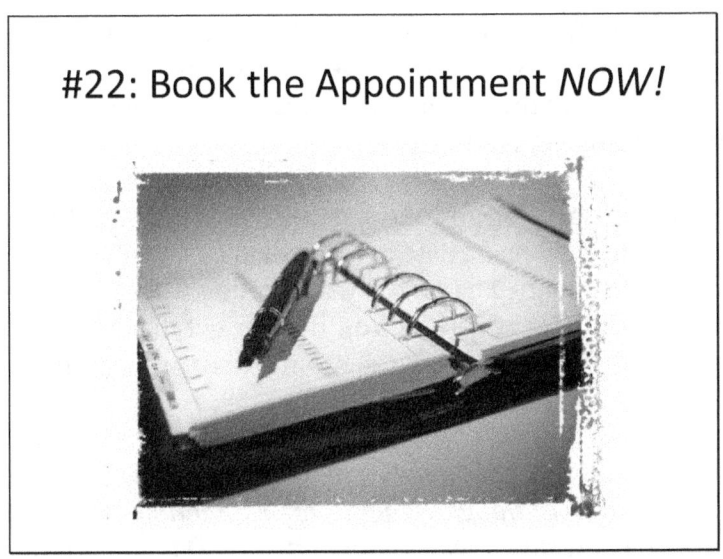

Typically, tax professionals close their seminar presentations by inviting anyone interested to call them later for an appointment.

That's a big, BIG mistake.

If you've done a good job motivating your audience, they'll never be more primed to schedule an appointment with you than they are right *at that moment*. It would be a shame to blow that connection by giving them some generic card or forgettable brochure and counting on them to call your office when they get back to theirs. So book the appointment right then and there!

If you have an assistant, bring them to the seminar. If you don't have someone to accompany you, bring your schedule. At the end of your talk, let your audience know that you have a certain number of appointments you can fill right there on the spot, and imply that you'll have to scramble to free up any more. Then sit back and wait for them to come to you – and leave the meeting secure in the knowledge that the appointments are on the books, rather than waiting and hoping.

A few years ago, one of our members gave his first seminar to a group of 15 real estate agents. I had coached him on this exact strategy, and he left that meeting with 13 new appointments. That's 87%! You'll *never* get that kind of success if you let them out the room without scheduling them.

John's Comment – Remember these are cut flowers, there are thousands of things vying for their attention. If they say they are interested book the appointment. Do not add steps, make it easy, make it fast, do it now!

#23: Video Sells!

When was the last time you saw one of your competitors using video to market his or her business? Never?

That's exactly why *you* should be using it yourself.

If you can't be there to talk to them in person, video is a powerful alternative. And contrary to what you might think, you don't need expensive equipment or high-end production values. These days, if you, or someone in your home or office has a smartphone, you have all the equipment you need to create effective video marketing materials.

Here are just a few ways you can use video to turbocharge your marketing and get new clients:

- Videotape yourself delivering a 30-second introduction for your website. Visitors will see you and hear your voice, building trust and rapport far faster than just seeing words on a page.

- Ask clients if you can record them giving you testimonials. Written testimonials are powerful (and we'll discuss them in more detail in Strategy #52). But if written testimonials are good, video testimonials are even better.

- If clients aren't comfortable delivering testimonials on camera, you can read their words to create video testimonials.

- Create a series of video "Q & A" sessions on frequently asked questions. Post the videos on your website to help establish authority and familiarity with visitors.

- Post your videos in a loop on a computer or tablet in your office waiting room. You'll create a more professional first impression than with a stack of old magazines on a coffee table.

- Create a YouTube channel and upload your introduction, your explanations, and your testimonials. Links back to your website will boost your search engine rankings, too.

John's comments – This has never been easier. We use software like Camtasia for higher quality stuff, but nothing is better than Loom video recorder for ease of use. Hit icon in browser and it will use your computers video and microphone, it saves in the cloud automatically and automatically creates a link, which you can post to Facebook or other platforms. Try to keep videos to about 3 minutes if marketing. Also, it is free. Check it out!

#24: Become an Author

Let's cut to the chase. Becoming an author is the single most effective thing you can do to get more clients (and better clients) for your business. Period. End of story. There's simply nothing else you can do to establish your expertise, credibility, and authority so effectively.

You can spend endless hours designing the world's best website. But *promoting* it costs thousands more. And if nobody *finds* it, you may as well not have done it at all. You can hire a slick ad agency to produce a gorgeous brochure. But brochures wind up in the trash. You can send thousands of letters or postcards, most of which will eventually land in the same place.

Or you can publish a book — hand it to prospects as tangible *proof* of your expertise — and watch their whole attitude towards you change. Right before your eyes, they'll stop seeing you as an annoying salesperson, and start seeing you as someone they should feel privileged to work with.

Books *impress* people. Books *wow* people. Books tell people that they can trust you with their toughest problem. Why? Because you're the guy who "wrote the book!"

Prospects don't even have to *read* your book to be impressed. (Seriously . . . most of them won't get past the introduction. That's fine. They don't have to actually *read* it to be impressed by you for writing it.)

"Yeah, yeah, yeah," you might be thinking. "That's all great . . . but who has time to write a book?" Well, if you're paying close attention, you'll notice that I said, "become an author," not "write a book." There are lots of ways to become an author without actually "writing" a book:

- You can hire a ghostwriter.

- You can license a book template to brand as your own. (The Tax Master Network has manuscripts you can cobrand.) In literally less than a week, you can be handing out books and enjoying the prestige of a book with your name and picture on it.

- You can collaborate with other authors and contribute a chapter to a group-authored book.

Becoming an author has more power to grow a new practice or reinvent an existing practice than anything else you can do.

John's comment – You can cobrand with Ed Lyon (like I am doing now). You can pay a service that allows you to cobrand with Brian Tracy, Steve Forbes and more. There are lots of options for every budget. Fun fact: The root word of authority is author.

#25: Books Instead of Business Cards

If becoming an author really is the most effective thing you can do to build your business (*and it is*), it follows that you want to promote your authorship as often and aggressively as possible. Copies are ridiculously cheap when you order in bulk, and at any rate, will be well worth the investment. Here are just a few to consider:

- Keep copies in stock at your office and invite clients to take them, to give to referrals.

- Bring copies to give out to everyone at your next networking meeting. (You *will* be asked to autograph them, and it'll feel pretty good!)

- Give away copies at trade shows where you exhibit for your target market. How much more credibility will you have as an author than as just another exhibitor?

- Give away copies to every prospect who schedules an appointment. Send them out as soon as prospects schedule those appointments, to impress them with your credibility before you actually meet them. Have your assistant call a couple of days after you send them out to make sure they're received.

- Send copies to meeting planners with offers to speak to their group. Offer to bring copies for everyone who attends. (Many meeting planners will actually *pay* for this arrangement — imagine actually getting *paid* to prospect!)

- Send copies to local reporters who might be interested in writing about *you* or interviewing you on air. Follow up with a list of five or six potential topics, with sample questions and answers.

- Send copies to your alumni magazines so your former classmates will see what an authority you've become. (If you spark a little envy from the loser that dumped you junior year, so much the better.)

- Give copies to your local libraries. Offer to appear and give talks for them.

- Talk up your book on your website. Invite online visitors to call your office for a free copy, even before they schedule an appointment. You can be sure they'll be more interested in meeting with you when they see what an expert you are than if you were just another business with a website!

#26: Get "Slightly Famous"

Americans are obsessed with celebrity. How else can you explain the success of those Kardashian girls who are famous simply for being famous? It follows, therefore, that your prospects will want to do business, when they can, with celebrities. And if you can make yourself into a celebrity – even a "slightly famous" local celebrity – that celebrity factor builds your business.

Celebrity gives you something called "social proof." Arizona State University professor Robert Cialdini, the author of *Influence: The Psychology of Persuasion*, defines this as the principle that "we determine what is correct by finding out what other people think is correct." When your prospects look around and see others doing business with you, that creates social proof.

Celebrity boosts social proof because the very fact of your celebrity means that other people are approving of your value. And celebrity also gives people a brag factor. It's one thing to say, "I got my plastic surgery done by some anonymous plastic surgeon in town." It's another thing entirely to say, "I got my plastic surgery done by the doctor who appears on *The Today Show*," or the local television news, or who creates their celebrity through their own local advertising.

Appearing on television and radio are the best ways to create celebrity. And just like "becoming an author," it doesn't have to be nearly as hard as you think. Consider these strategies:

- Hire a local publicist to get started. A month's retainer during tax season can run less than the cost of a modest direct-mail campaign.

- Compile a list of local reporters who might write about tax topics. Send them all copies of the book you authored after reading Strategy #24. (You'll be *amazed* at how fast the calls come in.) Add them to your monthly newsletter and weekly email list.

- Use an online press release service to distribute your own press releases.

- Buy airtime on local television or radio.

I published my first book, *The 60-Minute Tax Planner*, in 1998 and turned over my entire $7,500 advance to a publicist in Los Angeles. He got me two dozen national television appearances, dozens of radio broadcasts, and even an appearance on Roseanne Barr's short-lived talk show, where she introduced me as 'the funniest tax guy in America." It was without a doubt the best investment I ever made in my career. And the same sort of investment can work for you.

#27: Craft a Great "Elevator Speech"

Quick! Give me a reason why I should do business with you, in 30 seconds or less. Can you do it?

If you're like most tax professionals, you know exactly what an elevator speech is. You just don't *have* one!

"I'm a CPA" is *not* an elevator speech. That tells listeners what you *are*. But it doesn't say a thing about what you *do,* or why your listener should want do business with you.

"I do taxes" isn't an elevator speech, either. Yes, it tells listeners a bit more about what you do. But it doesn't tell them why they should hire you instead of anyone else. And it doesn't give them a beneficial reason for doing it now, as opposed to waiting 'til the last possible moment.

You want to dangle some sort of bait, in 30 seconds or less, that gets your listener to scratch their head and say, "hmmmm . . . I wonder how he does that . . . I want to learn more."

Let's say your "elevator-mate" is a doctor. Here are two approaches you might take to interest her in tax planning:

1. *"I work with doctors who are frustrated at their tax bill. They're disappointed with their current accountant and feel powerless to do anything to pay less. But you probably don't know anyone like that."*

2. *"We help you stop wasting money on taxes you don't have to pay. We do it in plain English, without intimidating spreadsheets or IRS gobbledygook. We tell you what to do, how to do it, and when to do it. It's all court-tested and IRS-approved. We'll even show you where the law says you can do it. You can use your savings for your retirement, your kids' college education, or even that dream vacation you've always wanted. The last doctor I worked with had organized his practice wrong and wasted $10,000 in employment tax that he didn't have to pay. I showed him how to reorganize his practice and stop wasting that money. He used the savings to install a home theatre in his basement!"*

The first example (which is straight out of the Sandler sales training system) focuses on pain and finishes with our own Strategy #45 (which Sandler dubs "negative reverse selling.") The second example focuses on the benefit to be gained. Either approach will be more effective than "I'm a CPA" or "we do taxes."

John's comment – If you haven't done this exercise, stop reading and do this now! You will have something to say, everywhere. My cocktail party speech (no one speaks in elevators, but the term is widely used). *"We help small business owners lower their personal income taxes."*

If they meet you, *"I'm a CPA,"* then meet me, who is more likely to get a card or a call later? This is back to my comment in #1, solution and value is the key. If I said I was a doctor and attorney most people would ask what kind, so the conversation would keep going.

The challenge with the CPA is no one really knows there are different kinds and their assumption about what you do is not helpful either. EAs have it worse, most don't know what it is. You need a hook to keep talking, work on it, refine it, and never stop changing it. Or steal mine, it works, and when I use it, I own the conversation. Or just say you are a Certified Tax Master, THAT will get their attention too, even if they have never heard of it.

Note: You have to become a Certified Tax Master if you want to say you are one.

#28: Pick a Smart Domain Name

Your website can be a great way to get new clients. But it won't be effective if visitors can't find you! Are you wasting your chance to make a great first impression online?

Tax professionals generally pick very bland domain names for their websites. If Jim Smith is a CPA, he probably picks something like www.JimSmithCPA.com. If that's taken, maybe he goes for Jim-SmithCPA.com, or JimSmithCPA.biz.

Bland domain names can cost you real opportunities to brand yourself. For starters, using your own name doesn't mean anything to visitors who don't already know you. And if your name is hard to spell, or your domain name includes a hyphen, or substitutes a number for a word (save4taxes.com), your intended visitor may never make it there!

You'll be much more effective using domain names that reflect the value you deliver to your clients, using words that everyone will recognize, and nobody will misspell. If you work in Chicago, for example, and you focus on tax planning, look for ChicagoTaxMaster.com, ChicagoTaxPlanner.com, or ChicagoTaxSavings.com.

Finally, like it or not, it's a dot-com world. Domain name registrars like GoDaddy.com want you to believe that extensions like .biz, .us, .ca, .tv. and .info are just as necessary as .com (Why? Because they're in the business of selling those extensions!) But none of those extensions command the same respect or recognition as .com. So if the .com you want is already taken, don't settle for a lesser extension. Find another name.

John's comment – I am about ready to expose a HUGE pet peeve of mine. It drives me nuts! Most of you already have a domain name (even if it is boring), I know this because you have a website, right?

But you still use a @AOL (nothing says "I'm outdated and old" like an AOL address) or @yahoo or even @gmail. It is free to forward any domain-based email address, so you can have you@taxpersonx.com forward to you@aol.com. It is unprofessional to have these old addresses if you own your own domain. Its free to have and give out a professional email. There is no excuse for it. Tax pros are supposed to be good at detail but miss this simple problem with their marketing.

One of the biggest complaints I get from tax pros is that they don't want to cobrand with, fill in the blank, and they send me the complaint from a poor brand them@aol.com account. Fix this now, join the 21st century!

I have now stepped off the 'soap box,' my rant is over and yes, I feel better.

#29: Create a Direct-Response Website

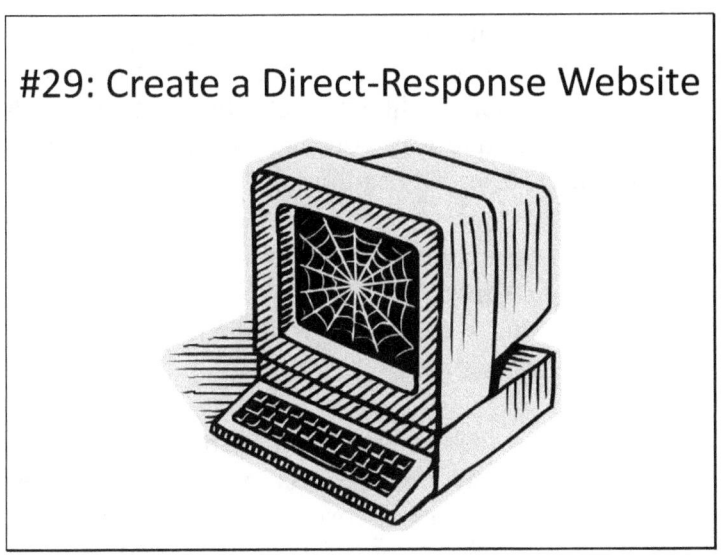

Getting visitors to your website is just half the battle. Once you get them, you need to keep them. Statistics show the average first-time visitor stays on a landing page just *eight seconds*. Does your website have what it takes to keep a prospect longer?

Most websites are bland, ineffective brochures. Up top there's a company name and maybe a logo. There's some happy-sounding pablum about the importance of relationships or putting people first. Somewhere near the bottom there's an invitation to subscribe to an emailed newsletter. But there's no call to action and no compelling reason to do anything besides leaving for YouTube and the latest cat videos.

The answer here is to create a direct-response website that keeps visitors from moving on to the cute cats, and motivates them to raise their hands and join your funnel. Here are the basics:

- The most important element on your landing page is your headline. You need a big, bold, benefit-oriented headline – something like "Here's How to Beat the IRS, legally." (Your name, or your firm's name, is *not* a big, bold, benefit-oriented headline.)

- The next-most important element is your picture. That's right, people want to see you, or you and your partners, or you and your staff. People want to see who they'll be doing business with.

- The next-most important element is the captions that accompany the pictures. Let's say you have a picture of yourself in the upper-left corner of your landing page (where your visitor's eyes will naturally land first). You can squander an opportunity by just dropping your name into the caption. Or you can command them to "call today to put my strategies to work for you!"

- You should include an opt-in box for your email list "above the fold" on the home page, where visitors will immediately see it. Don't just ask them to "sign up for our email newsletter" – nobody wants more email newsletters cluttering their inbox. Bribe them with an irresistible offer, like "Download our Free Report: 10 Most Expensive Tax Mistakes That Cost You Thousands."

- Make sure there are plenty of testimonials on every page. Video testimonials? Even better.

Designing effective web pages is a science all in itself. But these simple strategies will make your page at least twice as effective as it probably is now.

John's comment – This is a top of the funnel strategy. The more information you require the less 'leads' you will get, but that is OK. Quality beats quantity, you want to do the "cherry sorting" early on.

We like tangible books for this, it forces them to give us correct contact information, so we can mail it to them. We call the number they gave us first to verify authenticity, before we ship the book. This also avoids the common issue with "fake emails" that people use to get the free download.

Getting free reports on the internet is a great use for that old AOL account you love, now that you have followed my advice and have an adult emails address.

Sorry, apparently, I was not done with the rant...

#30: Give Prospects An Experience

Let's take one common frustration we've all faced. A prospective client calls for your "free consultation." You reserve an hour of your valuable time, hoping to convert them into a valuable client. But then they don't show . . . or even worse, they *do* show, pick your brain for an hour, then take your insights and ideas back to their old accountant to implement. How can turning your service into an *experience* convert more of those prospects into clients?

When prospects call to ask about your service, what do you do after you schedule their appointment? Do you just cross your fingers and hope they actually show? Or do you FedEx them a "shock and awe" package, with a copy of your book, a CD or an MP3 player with a recorded interview, a DVD of a speaking engagement, and a stack of client testimonials? Do you think something like that might impress them enough to guarantee they'll show for their appointment, and perhaps pre-sell them on your value?

When prospects show up at your office, do you have someone to greet them and show them to a couch with a stack of old magazines? Or do they get a scripted presentation, a tour of your office, and another stack of testimonials to review? Do you think making them feel like a VIP might get them more excited about your service than just parking them in the same waiting room they would find anywhere else?

When they finally sit down in front of you, do you give them a typical "consultation" and *let* them pick your brain for an hour, like they've always done with other tax professionals? Or do you walk them through some sort of structured "analysis," that *you* control, that finishes with a promise of immediate and measurable value that only *you* can deliver?

Selling tax services may not be "glamorous." But *choreographing an experience* for your prospects will help convert more of them into the kind of clients that build your business.

#31: Ask Provocative Questions

What's the best way to find out what a prospective client will buy? Ask them!

When you think "selling," you probably think about the things you should say to "close" your prospective client. But effective "selling" is actually more about asking questions and listening to the answers. You'll learn a lot more about your prospect – and specifically, what he or she is willing to buy – if you ask smart questions and listen carefully to the answers.

Asking provocative questions also works to drive a wedge between your prospect and their current tax professional. Here at the Tax Master Network, we talk about the "magic question": "When was the last time your tax pro came to you and said, 'here's an idea I think will save you money?'" The answer is almost always "never," and the question helps you start a conversation about how you're different.

Here are some more "wedge questions" to pose to your prospects:

- "Do you pay too much tax?" (Even prospects that don't pay tax at all will say yes to this!)

- "Are you happy with the taxes you pay? (Someone who says "yes" probably isn't a prospect for any more than basic tax-preparation service.)

- "Did you pay more tax this year?" (This is especially effective after April 15, for identifying prospects who might be unhappy with their current tax relationship.)

#32: Mouth Shut. Ears Open!

Once you've asked your provocative question, shut up and *listen!*

Too many of us think that "selling" means talking. Picture a "salesman," and you probably picture a fast-talking used-car salesman, razzle-dazzling hapless marks with a torrent of words until they buy. If that actually works, it's only because the marks realize that buying is the only way to shut the salesman up!

But effective selling isn't nearly as much about talking as it is about *listening*. Listen, and your prospect will tell you what frustrates him. Listen, and he will tell you what he wants. Listen long enough, and he will tell you what he's willing to buy.

If you're naturally a talker, this might be a challenge. You'll just have to resist the urge to blather on, even if you know in your heart of hearts that what you have to say is worth listening to. (I'm familiar with this challenge, being a talker myself. I would make a great parole officer because I never let anyone finish their sentences!)

If you're not a talker, then understanding that *effective selling is about listening* can be tremendously liberating. You don't have to worry any more about crafting a "pitch," or "trial closes," or "mirroring your prospect's posture." You can relax in knowing that you just have to start a conversation, and every word your prospect says will get you closer to a sale.

John's comment – Whether you are a talker or not if you combine this with the previous idea and create a list of well-designed questions that help you define what is important to the client you will be substantially ahead of your peers. This helps talkers because they need to get through the questions and talking slows down the process. It helps those that don't talk enough because they have a script.

Dan Sullivan's R-Factor question, it is a great opening question. The 'R' stands for relationship and helps you understand what they are hoping for, her it is. "If we were meeting three years from today—and you were to look back over those three years to today—what has to have happened during that period, both personally and professionally, for you to feel happy about your progress?"

I have altered this in many ways all with great results, it gets the conversation started and it focuses on what they want.

#33: Dangle Tasty Bait

When you're trying to sell your service, it's easy to get caught up in the "what" of what you do. You do taxes. You do writeup. You do payroll.

Maybe you do things differently than your competitors. You have an online payroll solution that lets clients enter employee timesheets in real time, which makes batching withholdings easier. Maybe you even do things *better* than your competition. You have a proprietary deduction-finding checklist that you walk your clients through at tax time.

Guess what. Clients don't really care about any of that. They aren't nearly so concerned about what you do as they are about why they should do it.

In other words, they don't care about the *features* you offer. They care about the *benefit* that is in it for them.

Too many tax professionals get caught up in the details of their processes. That's understandable – we're generally detail people making our living in a detail field. But clients don't care about the details. (That's why they have *you*.) They want to know what's in it for them.

By all means, go ahead and tell them about your whiz-bang deduction checklist. But don't ever assume they know why it's good for them. (Don't *assume* they can spell "tax" even if you spot them the "t" and the "a.") Tell them it puts more cash in their pocket – and then, if they ask, you can show off your process.

If you've followed the advice in Strategy #32 and *listened* to your prospect, you'll know exactly what bait to dangle. Some clients want the biggest possible refund. Tell them how you find "hidden" deductions other accountants miss. Some clients want convenience. Tell them how your evening hours let them get their returns done without missing work. Others worry most about audit plans. Let them know how your customer care program includes free responses to IRS inquiries.

#34: Make It *Hurt*

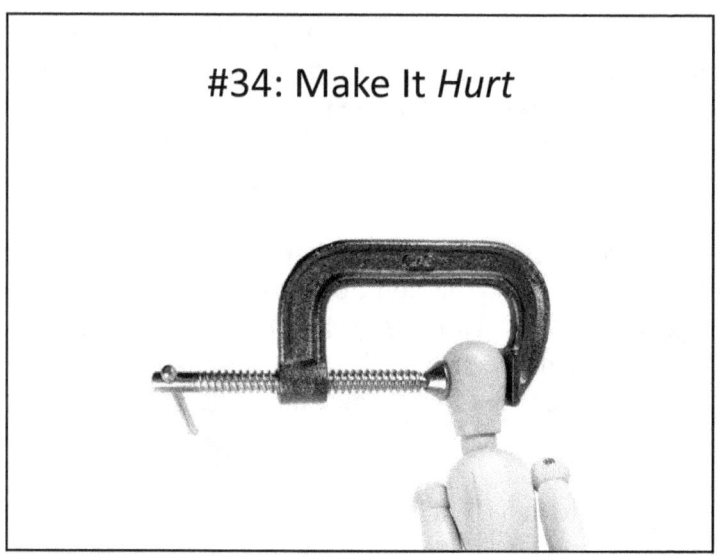

"The aim of the wise is not to secure pleasure, but to avoid pain."
Aristotle

Dangling tasty bait sounds like it would be the most effective way to motivate prospects to buy. But there's a flip side to that coin, and that flip side is even more effective. Read on and prepare to be surprised by a simple change in how you present the benefit of your service.

There are two ways you can motivate prospective clients for any "money" business. Pain, or gain. On Wall Street, they call it fear or greed. But really, it's all the same. And pain is by far the most effective of those two motivators. In fact, behavioral economists, who study the intersection between psychology and finance, tell us that pain produces twice the emotional impact as gain.

Try it for yourself: which of these assertions would make *you* act faster?

- Based on the information you've given me, I can save you $5,000 a year on your taxes.

- Based on the information you've given me, you're wasting $5,000 a year on taxes you don't have to pay!

Nearly all prospects will act faster on #2. Behavioral economists even have a name for it. It's called the "endowment effect," and it reflects the fact that we work harder to protect something we already feel is ours than we do to gain something we don't already have.

This is a lesson you can integrate into your marketing as soon as you put down this book, and in every conversation you have going forward. Pay attention, and you'll be amazed how switching your focus from "gain" to "pain" pays off.

John's comment – Pain avoidance is much higher value to people than virtually anything. The opioid addiction epidemic is due to desire for this pain mitigation. The massive insurance industry is pain avoidance (imagine the difficulty it would be to replace a house after a fire without insurance).

People want a hole not a drill bit. That simple analogy is important to understand in this discussion.

Most people are avoiding the pain of doing their own taxes, not a desire to have you do them. Keep that in mind.

#35: Find a Big Bad Wolf

Sometimes *selling* against some sort of obstacle or opponent is the best way to motivate prospects. Sometimes finding a "big bad wolf" is the best way to get them off the dime.

When it comes to taxes, this one is easy. Who's the big bad wolf? The IRS, of course!

Nothing unites like a common enemy. So find ways to help align yourself *with* your client, *against* the IRS, and watch revenues soar!

Consider these sorts of appeals for headlines, offers, and general conversation:

- We help you beat the IRS . . . legally

- We've got your back against the IRS

- We help keep the IRS out of your business

- We solve IRS problems

What do these all have in common? They don't appeal to your prospect's dislike of *taxes*. Taxes are an abstraction, and even the most anti-tax clients realize the government has to collect something.

Instead, they appeal to your prospect's visceral dislike of the *IRS*. They take a nameless faceless bureaucracy and make it into a big bad wolf.

The New York Yankees sell a lot of tickets when they play in Yankee Stadium in the Bronx. That's because New York fans love their Yankees. But the Yankees *also* account for big ticket sales in Boston when they play at Fenway Park. Why? Because Boston Red Sox fans *hate* the Yankees!

#36: Scare the Hell Out of Them

There are lots of emotions you can use to motivate prospects to act. We've already talked about appealing to their sense of gain, their sense of pain, and finding a big bad wolf. But don't forget appealing to their sense of fear.

Lots of tax-preparation clients are perfectly capable of sitting down and preparing their taxes themselves. They just don't want to. There are lots of reasons:

- Sometimes they just don't want to take the time. (I remember taking over tax prep for a doctor who had spent half a weekend the previous year trying to properly allocate income he had earned in New York and in Ohio to the appropriate state return. My software did the trick in literally no extra time at all.)

- Sometimes they don't want to learn how to do it. Even the self-guided interviews you find in tax-prep software have a learning curve. And taxes really are complicated

– I remember one member, who also works for Intuit, telling me the TurboTax maker wanted to take their online instructions from a fifth-grade reading level to a *third*-grade level.

- Sometimes, clients are just plain scared of the IRS. They might be perfectly capable of preparing their own return – but they want your signature there on the bottom just in case.

The IRS works very hard to project an intimidating image. That's why they announce prosecutions of lawbreakers like Pete Rose, Leona Helmsley, and Wesley Snipes around April 15. But your prospects don't know that the IRS launches a mere 5,000 criminal investigations every year. So they're afraid. (What gets people to church more often – the promise of heaven, or the fear of hell?)

Are you worried that you're somehow taking unfair advantage by using fear in your marketing? Don't be. Life insurance companies don't feel guilty when policyholders worry about dying. GEICO doesn't worry when customers worry about crashing. Colgate doesn't feel guilty when toothpaste buyers worry about bad breath. You're selling a service that puts their mind at rest. And you can take pride in delivering real value when you do just that.

#37: Make Them Laugh

News flash: taxes aren't especially entertaining. In fact, most people think they're boring. From there the stereotype has grown that tax professionals are boring, too.

Now, you and I both know this isn't true. Think about your college classmates, or your professional colleagues. They're just as entertaining as anyone else, especially when it comes to the ins and outs of the TEFRA regulations. And they're probably *more* entertaining than the attorneys and actuaries you know.

But that doesn't change the fact that your prospects expect you and your colleagues to be boring. Serious. Dull. Conservative.

Surprise them, and the increase in your business may surprise you. You don't have to be David Letterman or Jimmy Fallon. Just let a little personality and humor show through. Your prospects and clients will notice it. And they'll appreciate you for it.

You can use humor to reach prospective clients in all sorts of unexpected places:

- Humorous headlines grab attention and compel readership.

- Humor in presentations keeps their interest.

- Humorous stories make your point more effectively than dry "information dumps."

- Humor in seminars builds rapport with audiences.

Make sure you let your personality and sense of humor show through in *all* your communications, including your newsletter and weekly email. (See Strategy #57 for more information on staying on top of your clients' minds.)

#38: Create a Sense of Urgency

Give clients an opportunity to procrastinate, and they'll happily take it. Why put off until tomorrow what you can put off until the day after?

Everyone knows about April 15. But with so many clients taking extensions, even April 15 isn't the deadline it used to be.

The solution to the problem is simply to create an alternative sense of urgency to motivate them to act *now*.

Let's say you want to sell a tax-planning engagement to a business owner who files a Schedule C. It's June 1, and he's already filed his return. He's secure knowing that nothing matters for the better part of a *year*. Why should he feel any sense of urgency?

But his next quarterly estimate is due in just 15 days! How much more effective will you be if you tell him that you might be able to save him money in just two weeks?

If your prospective client operates his business as an S corporation, even better. His next paycheck may be *less* than two weeks away. And you can create that same sense of urgency before *every* paycheck.

For those of us in the tax planning business, December 31 is the biggest deadline of all. We have Tax Master members who bill more for tax planning in December than they do for tax preparation in April.

Here's the bottom line. If your prospect doesn't feel a sense of urgency to act, it's your job to light a fire under him. Do that now and you'll win clients who would have been perfectly happy to wait – or, worse yet, not act at all.

#39: Take Advantage of the Calendar

External influences make great conversation starters. That's because the other party doesn't have to start out by wondering where you're going – you both know what's up. There's always the weather, of course, but that doesn't start many tax-planning conversations.

Fortunately, you don't have to look any farther than the passage of time. The calendar is full of opportunities to open conversations about your service with your prospects:

- Late January attracts their attention as W2s and 1099s start to roll in.

- April 15 attracts attention, of course, even if prospects aren't ready to file just yet.

- April 16 attracts attention from prospects who feel stung by unexpectedly high bills or small refunds.

- July 4 attracts attention from prospects who love their country but feel they could be just as patriotic for half the price.

- "Back to school" attracts attention from parents who may soon have more time for tax planning.

- "Black Friday" attracts attention from bargain hunters who might be enticed into planning to pay less tax. (One of our most popular marketing resources is a "Black Friday" prospecting letter that asks, "What if the IRS had a sale?" and urges readers to come in for year-end tax planning.)

- Finally, December 31 is the hard-and-fast deadline for most annual tax planning, that even novices can appreciate.

Seriously – I challenge you to find me anything on the calendar that I *can't* turn into a pitch for tax services. Try it yourself, and you'll have a reason to talk about your services all year long.

John's comment – I mentioned earlier using the tax calendar, this is using the calendar as content for the lives people are living today. Mixing the two and you have a very robust marketing strategy. Now you need a top of the funnel 'product' like a special report on a webpage to collect email addresses. Are you seeing how the ideas can be mixed and matched?

#40: Take Advantage of the News

The daily news is full of conversation starters you can use to get new clients. You just have to keep your eyes and ears open for it!

- Is the Bureau of Labor Statistics reporting the economy is down? Now may be the right time to approach prospects for tax planning – if business is going to slow, then rescuing wasted tax dollars counts more than ever.

- Is the *Journal* reporting the stock market is down? Now may be time to talk with prospects about tax-loss harvesting.

- Has the IRS issued a ruling on bitcoin? Send an announcement to your clients letting them know you're ready to help with the new recordkeeping requirements.

- Has the tax Court issued a ruling that affects Medical Expense Reimbursement Plans? Send your eligible clients a quick letter explaining the new rules. (Our "Client Alert" feature automates this process and gives you a signature-ready letter to print on your letterhead and mail immediately.)

- Did your favorite NFL quarterback just sign a contract for a team halfway across the country? Clients may be interested in your take on how the higher state tax rate may actually mean less take-home pay.

You get the idea. Paying attention to the news, and relating it to your service, takes "taxes" out of the realm of the abstract and humanizes it for prospects. That, in turn, makes the sting of paying them hit closer to home – motivating prospects to act now.

#41: Make a Bold Promise

Back when my daughter Margaret was about 10, she had a joke she thought was pretty funny:

Q: *What does the shy pebble want to be?*
A: *Just a little boulder!*

Once you've got your prospect's attention it's time to hit him with an offer. Don't wimp out when it comes to calling him to action!

Studies show that the average American is exposed to 3,000 advertising messages per day. 3,000! And because we manage to ignore most of them, it takes a lot for a message to stand out. You won't wow prospects with wimpy offers that don't stand out.

For example, you can't just give a client a tax return. It has to be "expertly prepared, hand-reviewed, and computer-checked to give you the biggest possible refund allowed by law."

You can't just give a free consultation. It has to be "a free Tax Analysis," where you "find the mistakes and missed opportunities that may be costing thousands in taxes you don't have to pay."

I'm not saying you have to become a carnival huckster. I'm not saying you have to hype everything like a car dealer. But you do have to be bold enough to cut through the marketing clutter that surrounds your prospects.

Just be a little bolder!

John's Comment – This is an interesting one, because what if the truth is "too bold"? We ran a series of radio spots and advertised the Tax Blueprint® (a proactive tax plan) with a 3X guarantee. If you paid us $2k we guaranteed to get you $6k in tax savings this year or we would refund the whole fee. We didn't get a single call. We switched to our current 2X guarantee and the phone rang. Ironically, we were averaging a 12X return at the time, and we thought that was too bold (even though it was the truth).

I agree with being bold, but people have to believe it is attainable. The next idea will help with this.

#42: Give a *Strong* Guarantee

None of us like to think that our clients will be disappointed with us. You know who worries about that even more? Clients! One of the reasons clients don't do business with us – especially when it comes to services like tax planning that they've never paid for before – is their fear that they'll be disappointed and won't get their money's worth in whatever way they define that. If we can't convince them to risk their money on us, they won't say "yes"!

So, what's the answer? Take away that risk by offering them a strong guarantee. And make it clear to them that you're offering the guarantee exactly for that reason.

If an unhappy client comes to you and asks for their money back, you'll probably give it to them. You won't want to. You'll grumble and you'll resent it, right? But you'll realize that fighting it probably won't be worth the threat it poses to your time, your energy, and your reputation.

If that's how you feel about refunding an unhappy client, why not make it an integral part of your marketing? Why not distinguish yourself from the crowd, by offering a bold guarantee that your competitors would never think of offering?

Are you worried that clients will take advantage of you? I have yet to hear a single member tell me they regret offering a strong guarantee. Even if one or two clients do appear to abuse it, you'll more than make up for that with the host of new clients who are reassured enough to do business with you in the first place.

I've even told members to guarantee an initial *appointment*. Their websites say, "we guarantee it will be the best hour you spend on your taxes, or we'll donate $50 in your name to your favorite charity." I've encouraged this for half a decade or more, and not one member has ever told me they've had to make good on that offer.

#43: Give Emotional Reasons To Buy

You may think that saving your clients thousands of dollars in taxes they don't have to pay is enough to get their business. And in many cases, you'll be right. But some clients need more than just facts and figures to move. You have to give them an emotional reason to engage you.

In most cases, though, clients don't make decisions nearly as rationally as you think. They make decisions *emotionally*, *then* look for logical reasons to support those emotional decisions.

That's fine, as long as you know to give them that emotional reason in the first place!

The problem with dollars and cents is that, as impressive as they may sound, they're an abstraction. They're a means to an end. But to close a client, you have to link the means *to* that end. You do that by asking your prospect to spend the money – before you ask them to buy. (You'll need to remember Strategy #32 and *listen* after you ask.) Let's say you're talking with a business owner whose accountant told him not to bother with a home office deduction. You've taken a quick look at "the numbers" and determined that he's missing a couple thousand dollars a year in savings. He likes the idea of moving his business to you for the $2,000, but he's still not sold. What do you do?

Ask him what he'll do with that $2,000. Will he put it towards retirement? Will he use it to send his son to an awesome summer camp? Will he blow it on a week at the beach with his wife?

If he tells you he wants the beach, where will he go? Has he been there before? Does he have any particularly special memories of the place? You want him to hear the surf gently washing ashore. You want him to smell the tanning lotion and piña colada mix. You want him to feel the sand between his toes.

How much harder will it be for him to say "no" after you walk him through spending the money. Now, if he says "no," he's not just saying "no" to the $2,000. Now he's saying "no" to the beach, and the sun, and the steel drum band at night.

#44: Harness the Power of Stories

If you're a parent of a preschooler, I'll bet the last thing you do before you put them to bed is to read them a story, right? Your clients may be all grown up now. But there's still value in telling *them* stories, too.

Those of us in the tax business tend to think in terms of numbers. Numbers speak to our clients' analytical side. But they don't tug at our clients' emotions the way *stories* do.

Stories capture a listener's attention better than facts and figures – because stories take key facts and put them in an emotional context. And real stories, with heroes overcoming challenges, are far more effective with prospects than mere "data dumps." Which do you think will resonate with a prospect – a dry explanation of how S corporations work, or a success story about a client who established one and saved $10,000 in his first year?

Here's a quick formula for incorporating stories into your marketing and selling:

1. Grab your listener's attention with an unexpected challenge or question.

2. Give your listener an emotional experience by narrating your hero's struggle to overcome that challenge or answer that question.

3. Galvanize their response with an eye-opening resolution that calls your listener to action.

Take a few minutes right now to think about some client successes. Which of them can you turn into success *stories* to tell and re-tell to build your business?

#45: Know When to Push *Away*

Why does a high-school cheerleader play hard-to-get? Why does she make the quarterback sweat the invitation to the Homecoming Dance, even if she knows she'll say yes? *Because she can!*

You're not looking for a date to the dance. But you might find that playing hard-to-get helps grow your business. Picture this:

You've met a prospective client, at your office or theirs. You've walked through their tax return and identified mistakes and missed opportunities that cost them extra tax. Perhaps they're not taking advantage of a medical expense reimbursement plan. Perhaps they're missing opportunities to hire their children. Perhaps they're investing in taxable bond funds when municipals would make more sense. In any event, you discover you can save them money.

If you handle that part of your job well, you won't have to "close" them. They'll close themselves. But sometimes prospects do still resist.

When that happens to me, I'll bring out my "secret weapon." Sales trainer Dave Sandler called it "negative reverse selling." Marketing guru Dan Kennedy calls it "takeaway selling." But I call it "the high-school cheerleader" strategy, because you'll recognize it immediately as playing hard-to-get. Just hint that they *can't* have your service, or perhaps that they don't qualify. In many cases, that will eliminate their resistance.

> **Prospect**: "I don't know if this will really help me."
>
> **You**: "You're probably right. It sounds like taxes aren't really bothering you that much."

Alternatively, you might pull back a little and hint that you aren't even interested in working with him. Sometimes the best way to make someone want something is to tell them they can't have it!

Showing your client why they should want your service is the tax professional's equivalent of the cheerleader flashing her million-watt smile. Once you've established your value, you can play hard-to-get to take advantage of your prospect's natural desire to want what they're now afraid they can't have.

If you can show your prospect that your service and your fee are worth more than the taxes they would otherwise pay, then you can afford to play hard-to-get!

#46: "Close" Without Closing

Old-school sales trainers have dozens of "closes" they teach to make sales. There's the "Ben Franklin" close. ("Let's draw a line down the middle of this sheet, list the pros on one side and the cons on the other, and see which side wins.") There's the "assumed" close. (Talk as if the prospect has already agreed to buy.) There's the "thermometer" close. ("On a scale of 0-10, how likely are you to say 'yes' to this offer?")

The problem with most closes is that prospects have heard them. They sense when they're being "closed," and when it happens, their shields go up. Nobody wants to feel manipulated, and nobody wants to feel "sold."

The worst part is, we can't blame them for feeling that way because *we* hate feeling that way ourselves!

What's the solution?

Pick one "close" and stick with it. That way, you won't have to worry which close is the right one for any particular situation.

Pick something nonthreatening. It might be as simple as "what would you like me to do now?" or "where do you want to go from here?" Prospects who are ready to hire you will tell you to get started for them. Prospects who aren't ready to hire will still probably tell you what it will take to get there.

John's comment – The best close for non-closers is the 'assumptive close.' Just assume they are going to be clients and act like it. Break out the engagement letter as if they asked for it. It works, people want to be led and most hate change and decisions, make it for them.

#47: Give Prospects a Choice

Here's is a subtle psychological strategy to move prospects to "yes." Don't just ask them if they want to hire you or not. That sets up a choice between "yes" and "no" – and it's all too easy for them to say "no." Instead, give them a choice between two "yeses," and you'll find they choose "no" less.

Years ago, the kitchen retailer Williams-Sonoma offered a bread maker in their stores. They were doing pretty well with it, so they decided to offer a second, more expensive model. They figured if there was a market for bread makers at all, there might be a market for a more expensive, more profitable model.

They were gratified to see new sales for the more expensive model. But they had expected those sales to come at the expense of the lower-priced model. So imagine their surprise when they saw sales of that less expensive model actually go *up!*

The reason, of course, is that Williams-Sonoma had taken the old choice (between "yes" and "no") and replaced it with a new choice, between two "yeses."

Here at the Tax Master Network, we're big fans of monthly maintenance packages. You can offer clients a choice between packages, or a choice between a package and a flat-fee service. Either way, you grow your business faster by giving clients a choice.

#48: Tell Them How to Buy

You know how your business processes work because you manage them every day. But it's a mistake to assume that prospects know how they work, or even what to do when they decide to buy. That's why you have to make your calls to action clearly explicit, with step-by-step, "paint by numbers" explanations.

Have you lured a visitor to your website? What do you want them to do? Pick up the phone? Leave an email address? Or wander away without leaving any sort of contact information and hope they remember you again in six months when they need you?

Here are two actual calls to action I found online this morning. Tell me which one you think works better:

1. "Welcome to our website. Please take a look at the following sections we've created to help you reach your financial goals."

2. "Call me at 555-555-5555 and ask for your free Tax analysis. We'll find the mistakes and missed opportunities that may be costing you thousands in taxes you don't have to pay, then show you how our proactive planning service can rescue those lost dollars."

Obviously, #2 will get more action. You're telling your prospect what to do (call us), how to do it (555-555-5555), and the specific benefit they'll get from doing it.

The bottom line here is pretty simple. The easier you make it for prospects to buy – by not asking them to figure it out themselves – the more likely they are to say yes.

#49: Avoid the *Wrong* Offer

Sometimes, attracting the kind of client you want is as much about avoiding the wrong offer. Are you turning prospects off with tone-deaf offers?

A few years ago, we met a member from northern New Jersey who was looking to "upgrade" his practice, move away from the 1040 clients he had been serving, and start working with business owners. He brought us an ad to review that he had created for his local newspaper.

The problem was, he had designed his ad to look like a money-off pitch from the coupon section. There was the same dashed border you would see on a laundry detergent coupon . . . a bold headline offering "$25 Off of Tax Preparation" . . . and even an expiration date!

His offer might have been fine if he had been targeting price-conscious retail 1040 customers. But he wasn't. He was targeting affluent business owners. Not only were those business owners *not* looking for $25 off on their next tax return, the downscale message our member was about to send would have actually turned them off.

I met with another member outside Cleveland who was making a similar mistake. He had a sizeable 1040 practice and prepared 2,000 returns a year. He also wanted to build his business and financial services practice. Yet he was continuing to advertise that he would beat any national chain's price!

By all means, focus your marketing efforts on finding what your target market wants. But spend some time discovering what they don't want – and make sure you don't offer it!

John's comments – I did the $49 tax return business model for a couple of years, it is how I was exposed to the tax business.

I joke today that my lost leader strategy was all loss and no leader.

#50: Always *Ask* for Referrals

Now we'll spend the rest of our time together talking about referrals.

Everyone loves referrals. But hardly anyone does anything to *get* them.

I've had literally hundreds of members tell me their best source of new clients is referrals. Then I ask them, "what systems do you have in place to generate those referrals?" And I hear an awkward silence. I'm even more amazed at how many members tell me they never even *ask* for referrals.

If your service is good enough that clients send you all the referrals you need to grow, without even asking for them, congratulations. You're doing very, very well. But how much better do you think you'll do if you actually start asking?

Every conversation you have with a client is an opportunity to ask for referrals. You don't have to be obnoxious about it. Just remind them of something you've done for them, something they see as a benefit. (Even better if you can quantify it!) Then ask your client who they know, just like them, who would love that same benefit.

Let's say you've just shown a real estate agent client how to use a Medical Expense Reimbursement Plan to write off her daughter's braces as a business expense. Here's how the question might go:

> *"Who else at your agency does a pretty good business and also has kids at the orthodontist?"*

See? Easy, and subtle. Not intrusive, not obnoxious. *You* may know you're doing it, but your clients won't notice.

One final tip: When your client gives you a name, say, "Thanks, and who else?" Then shut up. You might be amazed how many good referrals you get from a single conversation!

#51: *Quantify* Your Value

Most tax professionals are pretty confident we do a good job for our clients. But very few of them know exactly how good they are.

Quantifying your value does wonders for your clients. They may like you. They may think you do a good job. But they don't really know, do they? Not unless you quantify it for them. Quantifying your value is a necessary step before you can communicate it to them.

And quantifying your value will do even wonders for you and your confidence. How will you know how well you do for your clients if you don't quantify it for yourself? Quantifying your value is a necessary first step before you can communicate your value to your prospects.

If you're like most tax professionals, you've grown blasé about your work and your value. You do things like recommend S corporations and set up medical Expense

Reimbursement Plans every day. You start to take yourself and your value for granted. And it makes you less effective in every aspect of your marketing and your work.

Quantifying your value is the antidote to taking yourself for granted. Quantifying your value restores your pride in your work. And quantifying your value boosts your confidence in a way that turbocharges your marketing.

A couple of years ago, I had a member in the office for a day of consulting. His goal was to restructure his billing to take his income from $900,000 to the magic million-dollar mark. I asked him to list his five best clients and write down exactly how much his service had saved them in taxes. After about 15 minutes, he told me the total was $2 million in one-time savings and $350,000 in annual savings. I asked him if he had *any idea* the savings were so great – and he said no. Then I asked him how he felt about it – and he said, "I'm pretty hot stuff!"

I had another member practicing in one of Chicago's affluent North Shore suburbs go through his top clients and find over $3 million in specifically identifiable savings.

How much more confident do you think those members were, approaching prospects and clients, after that exercise? How much easier do you think it was for them to approach prospects for new business and existing clients for higher fees?

John's comment – There are only two things small business owners want from their accountant. 1. Lower personal income taxes. 2. Numbers to help them run their business. Are you showing them regularly how you are doing that? If you are they will never leave, and they will refer you!

#52: Tell Clients What You're Worth

Now that you've quantified your value and you know what you're worth, it's time to tell your clients!

Telling your clients what you're worth gives them a reason to stay with you and a reason to refer you.

I've asked members over the years if they've ever sat down and told a client exactly what they're worth – exactly how much money they've saved their clients. Hardly any have ever done it.

Clients come to you for "the numbers," right? Well, how are they going to know how much you're worth if you don't tell them!

You don't have to be a braggart about it. Just a gentle reminder will do the trick. Slide a client his S corporation return to sign, and say, "Did you realize that since we switched you over to an S corp, you've saved $30,000 in tax?" Your client won't have realized it, of course, which is exactly the point of reminding him. Now you're not just "the guy who does the taxes.' Now you're "the guy who saved me enough to buy a boat," or even "the guy who saved enough to pay for my daughter's wedding."

If you thought quantifying your value felt great to you, imagine how it'll feel when you communicate it to your clients.

And that will be exactly when to ask for those referrals. "Who else just like you would be interested in that kind of savings?"

#53: Solicit Great Testimonials

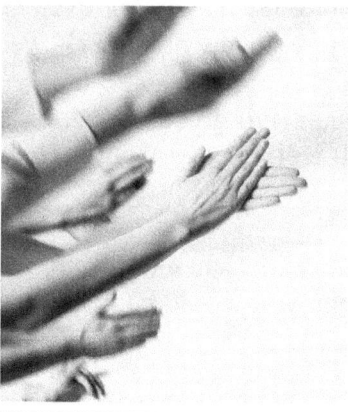

How many testimonials do you use in your marketing? If you're like most tax professionals, the answer is "none." And even if you are using testimonials, you're probably not using them enough. Online, for example, testimonials are gold. Google has recently upended traditional "search engine optimization" strategies by emphasizing online reviews, rather than key words and inbound links, for local businesses like your practice.

Gathering testimonials will probably be easier than you think. If your clients like you, all you have to do is ask! We recommend you create a simple one-page survey they can complete when they come to pick up their taxes or other work. Don't worry about asking them to rank you and your service on any kind of numerical scale. Instead, emphasize open-end questions like "what have you found most valuable about our service?" or "what would you tell a friend or family member who asked about us"? At the bottom, ask for permission to use their comments in your marketing material. Voila! Done.

Here are some suggestions for using those testimonials:

- Post them on your website.

- Post a link on your website promising "21 More Reasons" to use your service. Link to a page with 21 more testimonials.

- Include them in your brochures and other written materials.

- Make a stack of 20 or so that you can easily duplicate and mail out to prospects as part of a "shock and awe" package.

- Film yourself reading a testimonial and upload the video to your website and on YouTube.

Testimonials give prospective clients valuable "social proof" that they're making the right decision to hire you. And the act of asking for a testimonial is also a great time to ask for a referral. Just point to whatever you client cites as the biggest benefit you've given them and ask if they know anyone just like them who would like that same benefit.

You cannot ask for too many testimonials. You cannot have too many testimonials. You cannot use too many testimonials.

John's comments – There are some really great apps for this and some services that will allow you to build up 5-star reviews on google.

#54: Host Awesome Client Events

Admit it – at some point in your life, probably in college, you wished you could just party, all day and all night, for the rest of your life.

If you're reading this book, either you've changed your mind, or you never inherited that trust fund you were expecting. But you *can* still make parties a part of your business. In fact, you *should* do it three or four times a year!

Smart tax pros know that client appreciation events can be an inexpensive – and fun – investment in keeping your current clients and finding new ones. Just make sure you direct your clients to bring their family, friends, and colleagues as guests to your events.

Client events should be fun. They should be light and entertaining. You can give a couple of five-minute talks on hot tax or business topics. But don't turn the event into an extended seminar or sales pitch. The goal here is simply to spend "quality time" with your clients (thus giving them a reason to send you referrals) and introduce yourself in a low-key manner to their guests.

One of our longtime members lives in Temecula, California (California's "*real* wine country," as he calls it). One of his clients owns a vineyard. A couple of times a year, our member hosts a wine tasting at his client's vineyard. It costs about $1,000 for him to assemble about 50 clients, with an equal number of guests. And he converts about a third of those guests into new clients. You're an accountant, you can do the math.

Here are some more client events that members have hosted:

- A riverboat cruise down the Potomac

- A pig roast

- A museum tour

- A barbecue and hayride

- A "shredding party"

- A jazz concert

Use your imagination here. Let loose! Your clients will thank you for it, and talk you up long after the event itself is over. You'll find client events to be some of the smartest – and most fun – marketing you ever do.

#55: Be a "Connector"

Quick, what's the "golden rule"?

(No, it's not "he who has the gold makes the rules"!)

It's "do unto others as you would have them do unto you."

That suggests that if you want more referrals, you should start *giving* more. In fact, you should give until it hurts.

Legendary sales trainer Zig Ziglar once said that "you can have anything in life that you want if you just give enough other people what they want."

I say the bank that pays the highest interest is the Bank of Favors.

However you put it, the principle remains the same: do enough favors for others and they'll be bound to reciprocate with favors for you.

How many referrals have you given this year? How many have you gotten? If the numbers are roughly the same, does it make sense that *giving* more will lead to *getting* more?

Here's my "Connector Challenge." Resolve to make 100 referrals over the next year. That's just two referrals per week. Think you can handle it? If so, I guarantee you'll be amazed by the goodwill that comes back to you.

#56: Take A Client to Lunch

Let's say you have $5,000 to spend on marketing. Should you blow it all on a one-second Super Bowl spot? Maybe a direct-mail campaign? How about Google AdWords?

Nope, nope, and nope. Here's the best way to spend that $5,000.

Take a client to lunch. Do it twice a week for a year. That gives you $50 per lunch – enough for someplace nice enough to count.

(If you're new in business, you may not have 100 clients yet. That's ok – start with the clients you already have, then work your way "out" to other centers of influence and contacts who want to see your business grow. You'll get there soon enough.)

The referrals you pick up from those 100 lunches will *far* exceed whatever new business you would get from spending $5,000 on any cold marketing – direct mail, print, online, or anywhere else.

You'll also pick up more business from your existing clients. You'll learn more about them, their businesses, and their families. You'll learn what else they're willing to buy from you that they aren't already buying!

And, of course, you'll help keep your current clients longer. Don't underestimate how valuable that can be. If every client you had stayed with you just one year longer, how much more could you bill? How much easier would it be to keep your business growing?

You don't even have to go out to eat. You can cater lunch into your office, or have an assistant run out for it. Just make sure whatever you get is nice enough to flatter your client. You don't have to spend a fortune on a Michelin-starred meal – but nobody likes a cheapskate, either.

If you're worried about your time, have your client meet you at your office first so you can work right up until their arrival. Alternatively, bring an industry journal to read while you wait for them to meet you. They'll be impressed when they see you taking time to read for work.

#57: Stay on Top of Their Mind

Here's a crucial challenge any tax professional faces. Clients understand how important you are at tax time. But then they spend the rest of the year trying to forget you! You have to stay on top of their mind all year-round, lest they forget to come back next year. You also want that top-of-mind awareness any time a potential referral presents itself.

Fortunately, this is an easy problem to solve. And you can automate it just like I suggested in Strategy #4. You have two choices:

- You can mail a monthly newsletter. (Notice I said "monthly," not quarterly – if you're not going to do it monthly, you might as well not bother doing it at all.)

- You can send a weekly email. (Notice that for email, I said "weekly," not monthly – with email's lower open rate, if you're not going to do it every week, you might as well not bother doing it at all.)

But you can't mail just anything. Don't bore your clients with articles on "Three Ways to Make the Most of Your Depreciation Deductions," or "How to Open an IRA." Clients don't want to read that stuff – that's why they have you! Send something light, something personalized, and something fun.

Here at the Tax Master Network, we favor email broadcasts for several reasons. First, it's less expensive than printing and mailing a paper newsletter. Second, you can include all the prospects in your funnel at no additional cost. Third, it's more touches per year. Even if your recipient just deletes your email from their inbox, they've at least seen your name 52 times a year. (Nobody sends email from their tax professional to their spam box.) And fourth, email is easier – which means it's more likely to get *sent*.

Our "Networker" done-for-you email program, included in our Tax Master Network membership, is especially popular because the emails get *opened* and get *read*. We don't bore your clients with news from the latest tax Court decisions. We give them witty, engaging stories on topics like the tax consequences of Kim Kardashian's divorce, tax strategies for Somali pirates, and even tax strategies for a zombie apocalypse. (You probably never wondered how the government would collect estate taxes from the undead!)

For more information, visit www.TaxMasterNetwork.com!

John's comment – Tax strategies for the zombie apocalypse is a classic! This mixes a lot of the strategies already mentioned: humor, newsletter, cultivating the 'cherries.'

You have the raw ingredients, now create your favorite recipe.

PostScript

There you have it: 57 ways to get new clients, all wrapped up in a neat little bow. And hopefully, reading this little book has given you 57 more ideas of your own. (If not, that's okay – don't be surprised if you see us releasing *57 More Ways To Get New Clients* someday down the road!)

Now it's time to put the book to work. Ideas without action are worthless. I've given you the ideas. Now it's your turn to come up with the action.

Pick 3 ideas that you like best. Plan to incorporate them into your marketing. Then get out there and put them to work!

Maybe you'll add a video testimonial or two to your website, plan a client event, and start "researching" your target market's language. I don't really care which of the 57 ways you pick. Just *pick* them, and do something to *work* them. You'll probably be surprised with how far a little bit of effort can take you.

Once you're off to a good start, report back to me. Seriously. My email is edward.lyon@financialgravity.com and I'm always looking for feedback. The more I learn from you, the more I'm able to help you.

Finally, if you haven't already done so, visit me online at www.TaxMasterNetwork.com. You'll find at least 57 more ways to grow your business, along with a unique online tax-planning system and a national community of tax business marketers sharing what works. We'd love for you to be a part of it!

www.ingramcontent.com/pod-product-compliance
Lightning Source LLC
Chambersburg PA
CBHW072144170526
45158CB00004BA/1497